AFRICAN ETHNOGRAPHIC STUDIES OF THE 20TH CENTURY

Volume 11

ANTHROPOLOGY IN ACTION

ANTHROPOLOGY IN ACTION

An Experiment in the Iringa District of the
Iringa Province Tanganyika Territory

G. GORDON BROWN AND A. MCD
BRUCE HUTT

LONDON AND NEW YORK

First published in 1935 by Oxford University Press for the International African Institute.

This edition first published in 2018
by Routledge
2 Park Square, Milton Park, Abingdon, Oxon OX14 4RN

and by Routledge
711 Third Avenue, New York, NY 10017

Routledge is an imprint of the Taylor & Francis Group, an informa business

© 1935 International African Institute

All rights reserved. No part of this book may be reprinted or reproduced or utilised in any form or by any electronic, mechanical, or other means, now known or hereafter invented, including photocopying and recording, or in any information storage or retrieval system, without permission in writing from the publishers.

Trademark notice: Product or corporate names may be trademarks or registered trademarks, and are used only for identification and explanation without intent to infringe.

British Library Cataloguing in Publication Data
A catalogue record for this book is available from the British Library

ISBN: 978-0-8153-8713-8 (Set)
ISBN: 978-0-429-48813-9 (Set) (ebk)
ISBN: 978-1-138-49215-8 (Volume 11) (hbk)
ISBN: 978-1-351-03098-4 (Volume 11) (ebk)

Publisher's Note
The publisher has gone to great lengths to ensure the quality of this reprint but points out that some imperfections in the original copies may be apparent.

Disclaimer
The publisher has made every effort to trace copyright holders and would welcome correspondence from those they have been unable to trace.

ANTHROPOLOGY IN ACTION

AN EXPERIMENT IN THE IRINGA
DISTRICT OF THE IRINGA PROVINCE
TANGANYIKA TERRITORY

By

G. GORDON BROWN, M.A., Ph.D.

and

A. McD. BRUCE HUTT, B.A. (OXON.)

With an Introduction by
P. E. MITCHELL, C.M.G., M.C.
CHIEF SECRETARY, TANGANYIKA
TERRITORY

WITH 1 MAP AND 4 APPENDICES

Published for the
INTERNATIONAL INSTITUTE OF
AFRICAN LANGUAGES & CULTURES
by the OXFORD UNIVERSITY PRESS
LONDON : HUMPHREY MILFORD
1935

OXFORD
UNIVERSITY PRESS
AMEN HOUSE, E.C. 4
London Edinburgh Glasgow
New York Toronto Melbourne
Capetown Bombay Calcutta
Madras Shanghai
HUMPHREY MILFORD
PUBLISHER TO THE
UNIVERSITY

PRINTED IN GREAT BRITAIN

PREFACE

THIS monograph is the outcome of an experiment made by the authors in an attempt to discover to what extent anthropological knowledge can be made applicable to the problems surrounding the administration of an African tribe. The experiment was carried out over a period of one year, amongst the Hehe tribe, who inhabit the District of Iringa, in the Iringa Province of the Tanganyika Territory. One of the authors, Mr. Brown, has been doing anthropological field-work among the Hehe since August 1932, and, in a previous expedition, from March 1930 to July 1931. The other author, Mr. Hutt, has been District Officer of the Iringa District since May 1932. They are referred to in the monograph as the anthropologist and the administrator respectively.

The conduct of the experiment and the writing of the monograph is a joint effort throughout; but the information and the opinions given in Chapters II and III are the responsibility of Mr. Brown alone. Both authors accept responsibility for the opinions expressed and the conclusions reached in Chapters I and IV.

The authors wish to acknowledge their indebtedness to Mr. P. E. Mitchell, C.M.G., M.C., Secretary for Native Affairs[1] in the Tanganyika Territory. It was he who originally suggested the experiment; his assistance and advice have been of great value

[1] Now Chief Secretary.

throughout its course and during the writing of the book; and the authors feel that the value of the latter has been materially enhanced by his Introduction.

Mr. Brown also wishes to acknowledge his indebtedness to the Rockefeller Foundation, whose assistance made possible both his expeditions to the field; to the International Institute of African Languages and Cultures, who generously assisted his second expedition; and to his wife, Elizabeth Fisher Brown, who has been associated with him in all his field-work, and who has collected much of the material utilized in these pages.

It will be noted that, in the descriptive chapters, facts are given without the proof or the corroboration which are ordinarily expected in an anthropological monograph. Both during the preliminary part of the experiment and when writing the book, it was considered more profitable to state facts as simply as possible, leaving the proofs for further publications. The essence of the experiment was the presentation of useful facts to a non-specialist, that he might apply them to current requirements; and the presentation of masses of proofs would have complicated matters unnecessarily.

G. GORDON BROWN.
BRUCE HUTT.

December 1934.

PHONETIC NOTE

No attempt is made in this book to give exact phonetic symbols. The vowels are as in Italian. Of the consonants, *g* and *k* are frontal, the sounds approximating to *j* and *ch* respectively, when followed by the vowels *e* or *i*. *l* is cerebral, *v* is bilabial, and the others are as in English. The symbols *ng'* for *ŋ* and *ch* as in English have been retained, on account of their widespread use in East Africa.

CONTENTS

PREFACE BY THE AUTHORS	v
INTRODUCTION	xi
I. THE NATURE AND METHOD OF THE EXPERIMENT	1
II. THE HEHE TRIBE	20
A. SOCIAL ORGANIZATION	23
1. Political Organization	23
(*a*) The Tribe	23
(*b*) The Chief	28
(*c*) The Sub-Chiefs	44
(*d*) The Headmen	57
(*e*) The Subject	79
2. Kinship Organization	82
(*a*) The Family	83
(*b*) Marriage	97
(*c*) The Public Regulation of Family Life	115
B. LAW	120
C. LAND TENURE	127
D. ECONOMICS	134
E. RELIGION	166
F. OTHER CUSTOMS	172
1. Stories and Traditional Histories	173
2. Magic and Witchcraft	175
3. Female Initiation	184
III. THE CHANGING TRIBE	190
A. ADMINISTRATION	192
B. TAXATION	201
C. EUROPEAN LAW	205
D. NEW RELIGIOUS BELIEFS	209
E. EDUCATION	215
F. EUROPEAN SETTLEMENT	220
IV. CONCLUSIONS	223

CONTENTS

APPENDICES

    A. Specimen Native Court Warrants . . . 241
    B. Skeleton Native Treasury Budget . . . 245
    C. 1. Classified List of Questions . . . 249
        2. Answer to Question No. 23 . . . 255
        3. Answer to Question No. 33 . . . 257
        4. Answer to Question No. 64 . . . 263
    D. List of Tribes prior to Amalgamation . . 265

INDEX 269

    HEHE WORDS AND PHRASES . . . 271

INTRODUCTION

My Dear Hutt,

On my recent visit to Iringa you and Gordon Brown and I had some discussion about a proposal I made to you some time ago that you and he should make a practical experiment in co-operation between a District Officer administering his District and an anthropologist carrying out research work in it. You have already put the proposal into practice to a certain extent, and in order to give it a more definite form you have asked me to outline it for you on paper. I will try to do so.

In the field of what is commonly called native administration a policy of local government has been adopted in Tanganyika designed to provide the framework within which the administrative, social, and economic progress of the people might be promoted from foundations resting on their past, compatible with their present, and suited to their future.

It is important in relation to the work which you propose to do to understand clearly the implications of this policy, which may be very briefly summarized by saying that it aims at an administrative system deriving from and resting on local organizations, loyalties, and traditions, but compelled by the supervision of a trained British staff to assure to the people proper standards of security, honesty, justice, and efficiency. It cannot be static, but must always be capable of development or modification; it is a means, and not an end, a means of achieving at least certain minimum requirements; and if it fail in that, it is for the British staff to take the steps that may be judged necessary.

In the first phase the task of the administrative officers has been threefold. They had first to seek the information which must be obtained before such a policy could be launched, and to submit to their superiors detailed plans suited to the circumstances of each area and tribe. Secondly, they had to establish and guide the system, and even to operate it in cases where beginnings were weak. Thirdly, they had to ensure that the local administrations were kept within the limits imposed by Government policy and relevant legislation and that the results did not fall short of permissible standards.

It was not, as some seem to have thought, a case of discovering old forms or establishing and supporting tribal chiefs as an end in themselves, nor of riveting outworn or outwearing institutions on an ignorant people before they were able to outgrow them; nor was it a case of king- or constitution-making, of inventing a system and imposing it from without as something which the British officers had decided would serve their purpose.

The administrative officers performed their task with remarkable skill and a great measure of success, but mistakes were inevitable and in some cases steps had to be retraced or diverted, with as little apparent disturbance as possible, to other paths. In any case, it was seldom possible to do more than set up the bare framework, leaving the rest to be filled in as the passage of time and the growth of experience suggested. For this the fullest knowledge is necessary, knowledge not of a definitely ascertainable static condition but of the circumstances and effects of past acts and of existing conditions and tendencies.

But administrative officers, especially District Officers, have a multitude of duties, and their executive functions are so numerous and so complex that it is seldom possible to combine them with research; moreover, men placed in positions of such peculiar responsibility and authority among a backward people are under certain special disabilities in prosecuting inquiries of this nature.

You and Brown agreed with me that there would be valuable experience to be gained from a practical attempt to solve the difficulty by linking specialist research to the day-to-day business of administration, in a manner which might be compared to the relation between laboratory worker and practising doctor, and that an attempt of this nature would have to be confined in the first place to a limited field and to proceed experimentally towards the discovery of methods capable of general application.

Thinking on these lines I have formed some rather tentative views on the subject which I set out below in deference to your request.

It is impossible to imagine circumstances which would enable a Government to provide each District with its own research worker. If these methods prove capable of general adoption, a condition will evidently be that the research worker will be at the disposal of Districts in turn, and then only for limited periods. A limitation would, therefore, be imposed upon the degree to which each subject for investigation should be analysed, and care would be needed to avoid excessive detail which would make the method unworkable.

An attempt of this nature, which might be described as an experiment in applied anthropology, would be best made in a field restricted to one administrative district inhabited by a single tribe. The choice would not fall on one of the more backward districts, for there conditions might not be typical nor would the time-factor be so pressing; nor on one of the most advanced, for there the complications might be so numerous as to endanger the whole experiment and obscure the broad lines which must be followed at the first attempt. A typical district, therefore, midway between these extremes would offer the most suitable field.

Such a district is Iringa, where in addition chance has brought you and Gordon Brown together; you seem to me to make a combination admirably qualified to try new methods and to get the most, and the most reliable, results from the experiment.

The task is twofold, and may be summarized in two questions: (i) is the local government based on tribal loyalties and traditional authority, deriving from the past, acceptable in the present, and, as far as can be judged, capable of appropriate development to meet future conditions? and (ii) are the people well governed and content?

The first step might be to obtain a general historical account of the tribe, its origins, traditions, and organization, to be followed by a description on the broadest lines of the political, economic, and social conditions in which it finds itself to-day, and the administrative structure, British and native, set over it. A comparison might follow of the old tribal hierarchy with the existing administrative and judicial organs, showing differences and if possible accounting for them. Answers would be sought to the questions: Are such differences due to the overriding requirements of a European central government? Or to natural developments to meet changed conditions? Or to distortion, intentional or unintentional, by local British officers, or by a chief seeking greater power for himself, or by sub-chiefs, headmen, or elders, exploiting the weakness or indifference of a chief?

These inquiries might be regarded as an examination of the means, and investigation would follow into the measure of success in achieving the desired end. This would necessitate an attempt to formulate with some precision what the end should be, and here a distinction between immediate and distant objectives would emerge.

Modern conditions involve the substitution for a subsistence economy of personal property, profit, and the measurement and exchange of wealth by a standard which we call money. A modern Government necessitates the collection of revenue in money and the payment of salaries to at least the majority of those who discharge public functions. Taxation must therefore come under review in relation to the economic capacity of those who have to pay it, as well as to methods of collection and their effects on individuals and society. Answers would be sought to questions such as the degree of efficiency and the extent of corruption in the assessment and collection of taxes, and the consequences of the substitution of paid officials for officiating tribesmen. The larger issue of the economic basis and potentialities of peasant agriculture in local conditions can hardly fail to emerge; and employment for wages, trading, and other economic activities would be brought in review, not only as a measure of the scale and incidence of existing taxation, but also for the not less important purposes of assessing their effects upon present conditions of life and of planning for the future, for clearly such planning must be meaningless unless it is related to the general level of wealth which it is reasonable to anticipate.

It may be assumed that the natives of Tanganyika will have to build their future, as their present is based, upon the productivity of their land. The manner in which they now hold and use their land and developments from past practice would, therefore, be an important line of inquiry.

The powerful religious forces which foreign races have brought to bear upon the natives could not be omitted from such an investigation, at least in their direct social effects upon such fundamental things as marriage and relationship, and personal status. Such inquiries would bring into the picture the customary law of the people and the developments and modifications which it is undergoing by the impact of these new forces, or the actions, deriving from them, of missionaries or legislators. This again would involve a comparison of native and foreign sanctions and their effects upon individuals and society.

I have attempted no more than an outline, but it shows the task to be formidable and extensive. All of it may not be fulfilled, but in attempting it valuable data should be obtained for future attempts and useful experience of what may perhaps be described as the technique of putting the results of research into current use. Part of the inquiry might be found to fall naturally into place as the preliminary work which Brown, as an anthropologist, would wish to complete before addressing himself to a study of present conditions, and as the background from which you as the responsible administrator would approach the practical difficulties of the day. This part would be historical and descriptive in form, and it might be an advantage if anthropologist and administrator could collaborate here to produce an agreed statement. Thereafter it would be for the administrator to ask questions, and for the anthropologist to answer them. It must clearly remain the responsibility of the administrator to decide whether to act or intervene in consequence of information so obtained, but he would be careful not to dispute, or be drawn into argument about, its correctness, for that is the responsibility of the anthropologist. The anthropologist for his part would abstain from expressing agreement or disagreement with the actions of the administrator, but not from describing their effects; he would not advocate or condemn particular courses, though he would describe their advantages or faults; his principal concern would be to answer to the best of his ability the questions put to him.

It may be objected from the administrative side that division of authority and responsibility, or delay and uncertainty in administration, will result from a general application of this method. To anthropologists it may seem that intolerable restrictions upon their freedom of action and expression must result, and that considerations of expediency will not fail to influence research. The work you have undertaken claims to be no more than an experiment, however, and only by experiment can such objections be answered. We have discussed the project at length, and I have personally no doubt that it will be attended by a great measure of success and will provide lessons of permanent value in this field. I wish you and Brown every success, confident that the task could not be placed in keener or more competent hands.

Yours sincerely,

Dar es Salaam.   P. E. Mitchell.

I
THE NATURE AND METHOD OF THE EXPERIMENT

GENERALLY speaking, there is no doubt that properly directed anthropological research could be of great practical value in the administration of primitive peoples. Unfortunately, in the past, there has been a tendency to regard it as being too academic to be of any immediate use. The experiment undertaken at Iringa and described in this monograph is an endeavour to discover to what degree and in what manner anthropological knowledge can be acquired and applied to the problems of native administration.

The essence of the experiment was first to discover what fields of knowledge were of use to the administrator, and secondly to evolve a simple method of securing and presenting such knowledge in a way that would serve immediate practical ends. That previous attempts to do so have not always been fruitful, is due partly to certain prejudices. The anthropologist has been regarded at best with a kindly tolerance by the practical man; and the practical man has often been looked upon with academic scorn for his disregard of the minutiae of native custom by his more scientific colleague. In short, it was a failure to recognize that, in many fields of activity among primitive people, the work of the administrator and the work of the anthropologist could become complementary and that each had much to learn from the other, that has been the cause of the gap between theory and practice. In addition to such unfortunate, if natural, prejudices, the fact must also be borne in mind that systematic attempts to work out a basis of co-operation are rare. The anthropologist is apt to assume that the presentation of his published results will be of use if read by the administrator concerned, but frequently has in mind the bearing of his results on problems of general theory, rather than on those of practical necessity. Sometimes, also, his results are published after the conditions he has described have altered considerably. The administrator, on the other hand, reading in current anthropological literature much that he considers irrelevant to the problems in which he is engaged, may not recognize the presence of much that is relevant, and may therefore sometimes dismiss the whole of anthropology as unpractical.

These statements may be extreme. They might suggest that all the valuable research work done in the past by government anthropologists, working under government auspices, and by anthropologically trained government officials, has been useless practically. They might also suggest that even if such past researches have been potentially useful, their value has never been recognized by the practical men concerned. We do not intend such sweeping suggestions, and to do so would be unjust, not to say impertinent. But we do think that our statement of the attitude adopted by administrators is true on the whole, allowing for a number of exceptions. And we do consider the reason to be that, in the past, research has generally been too academic and not closely enough related to practical needs. In any case, there are few, if any, records of close co-operation between anthropological theory and administrative practice; and the application of anthropological research to current problems of administration is still in an experimental stage.

The present attempt at collaboration was, from the beginning, based on the assumption that anthropologist and administrator could be of use to each other, but that the method of co-operation had yet to be devised. The key to the present approach has been stated by Professor Malinowski: 'The practical man should be asked to state his needs as regards knowledge on savage law, economics, customs and institutions; he would then stimulate the scientific anthropologist to a most fruitful line of research, and thus receive information without which he often gropes in the dark.'[1]

The present experiment is an expansion of much that lies implicit in that sentence. At least two problems require elaboration: to evolve some criterion whereby the administrator may 'state his needs' and not merely satisfy an idle curiosity; and to evolve some method of presenting results which will include all that is relevant, and exclude all that is irrelevant, to the problems formulated. To these problems we

[1] Bronislaw Malinowski, 'Practical Anthropology', *Africa*, vol. ii, no. 1, Jan. 1929, p. 22.

add a third, that of assigning to the anthropologist and to the administrator each his proper task. The main lines of each man's role are laid down by the very nature of the experiment; but it is important to delimit it more accurately. The administrator has the immediate and constant task of making practical decisions; the anthropologist has an interest in the decisions made, but should refrain from criticism in case of a difference of opinion, once he is sure that the administrator has all the relevant facts. The anthropologist, on the other hand, is in a position to obtain more accurate information; the administrator must accept the information as given, even if it necessitates an unexpected change in his plans. Efficient collaboration can only exist if each man loyally accepts the prerogative of the other in his own sphere; and it is not an easy matter to draw up the terms of such collaboration, while at the same time maintaining an honest and effective co-operation.

The experiment was made in the Iringa District of the Iringa Province of Tanganyika. Circumstances irrelevant to the main issue decided the place, since one of the authors was the District Officer and the other had been for some time engaged in anthropological work in that area. Fortunately it happens to be a good District in which to make such an attempt. First, the tribe inhabiting the area, the Hehe, are typically Bantu; that is, their social organization and their customs do not deviate unusually from those of other Bantu tribes. Secondly, they may be taken as average in their degree of sophistication: they are not so advanced as some of the coastal people of the territory, nor are they so primitive as other tribes more remote from, or more impervious to, European influences. And thirdly, there are a number of European settlers and two missions in the District, as well as several trading centres; the effects of the impact of foreign races on the tribe can thus be studied in close perspective.

The Iringa District has an area of nearly 12,000 square miles, with a native population of 86,795 according to the 1931 census. The bulk of them live on a plateau at an altitude of between 4,500 and 7,000 feet, while the remainder inhabit the plains in the north and east, at an altitude of about 2,500 feet. Their basic economy is agriculture; maize is the staple crop, though millet or rice predominates in some of the low-lying areas. They have as subsidiary crops eleusine, beans, potatoes, ground-nuts, and marrow. They also possess cattle, and, to a less extent, sheep and goats; but live-stock is a secondary source of wealth, since there are only 120,000 head of cattle in the whole tribe, rather less than two per head of population.

The tribe was not subject to direct European influence until the end of the last century. The first German expedition sent against it was practically annihilated in 1891; the second expedition in 1894 destroyed the capital, Ilinga (now Kalenga); in 1898, the last independent paramount Chief, Mkwawa, committed suicide to avoid capture; and from that event we may date its complete conquest. The tribe has been ruled since 1926 by Chief Sapi, who is the son of Mkwawa.

The township of Iringa is situated 162 miles from the railway, to which it is connected by a section of the Great North Road. It is the administrative head-quarters of the District, with an administrative staff consisting of the District Officer and two Assistant District Officers. In addition, there are a Government Doctor, a Nursing Sister, two Police Officers, a Veterinary Officer, a Surveyor, a Telegraph Inspector, and an Officer of the Public Works Department. The Provincial Commissioner of the Province also has his head-quarters at Iringa, while Officers of the Agricultural, the Forest, and the Education Departments are stationed in different localities outside the township.

There are 376 Europeans in the District, the majority of whom are engaged in farming, and 315 Asiatics, chiefly traders and artisans. Christian missions are represented by the Italian Consolata Fathers (Roman Catholics) and the Berlin Lutherans. The former have their head-quarters at Tosamaganga, some 12 miles west of Iringa, while the head-quarters of the latter are at Pommern, 40 miles to the south-east.

This, in brief, was the material which we set ourselves to study. At the outset, we were confronted with a threefold problem: to assign to each collaborator in the experiment his proper role, to determine the extent and limits of anthropological knowledge relevant to administration, and to evolve a scheme of presenting such knowledge. The method which was finally adopted, after several alternatives had been discussed and rejected, will emerge more clearly in the succeeding pages. It may be summarized by saying that the administrator was to ask the anthropologist questions concerning his practical problems as they arose, and that the anthropologist was to limit his answers by a consideration of the particular circumstances which gave rise to the questions. The adoption of this method obliged us from the beginning to reach a definite understanding of the nature of the questions, and we accordingly formulated the following categories, within one of which each question must fall:

   (i) Questions of fact pertinent to the practical problems concerned.

  (ii) Questions as to the probable consequences of a projected course of action.

 (iii) Reports upon the effects of measures which had already been adopted.

For instance, during the course of the experiment, the administrator had under consideration the desirability of advising the Native Authorities[1] that marriages and divorces should be registered by the Native Courts.[2] The anthropologist was accordingly asked (i) for relevant information concerning native marriages and their dissolution, and (ii) for his opinion

---

[1] See below, p. 11.
[2] See below, p. 11.

of the practicability of enforcing registration and of its probable consequences. In a few years' time, the anthropologist could also be asked for information about the actual consequences of this measure.

The questions to begin with were specific and limited; it was realized from the first that, eventually, a large field of native custom must be covered, but that the more specific the questions at first, the more accurately the broader fields of relevant interest would be indicated. After the first few questions were asked and answered, more general questions were, in fact, asked; but by that time, both the collaborators were surer of their ground, and the relevance of the questions to the problems of administration were more easily seen. For example, the first three questions (chronologically) referred to the registration of marriages and divorces, the extent of polygyny, and the effect of capital punishment as a deterrent to murder. Later, questions covered such comprehensive topics as witchcraft, the principles of native law, and questions of political organization. But the specific and limited questions always outnumbered the general ones; and this is considered an advantage, in that it not only yielded answers of immediate practical utility but kept the more general questions closer to the administrative necessities from which they originated.

Early in the period of collaboration, it became apparent that it was necessary to formulate with some precision the functions and duties of an administrator and the knowledge he should possess to enable him to discharge them. From this analysis, the administrator was able to determine more precisely the range and scope of his questions and the criteria of what was to be included and what excluded from the survey. The final decision of what information was to be asked for was left by agreement to the administrator. Throughout the experiment, the anthropologist tended to press for the inclusion of a larger body of knowledge than the administrator thought necessary; some disagreements arose on this point, which could only be decided on the basis of an agreed principle; and the principle finally adopted was whether, in the administrator's opinion, the information in question would or would not enable him to discharge more efficiently his tasks as analysed. The analysis which follows has thus a very direct bearing on the problem of formulating useful questions.

The administrator has, in the first place, to give effect to the policy and legislation of the central government and to be guided in all his actions by what may be described as the general aims to which that policy is directed. Secondly, he has to supervise and control the executive and judicial organs of the native administration, to see that they conform, on the one hand, to policy and legislation, and that, on the other, they afford proper standards of security of person and property, of justice and honesty, and do not fall short of the degree of efficiency in practice which is necessary in the day-to-day business of administration. He has constantly to reconcile the insistent practical demands of the moment with possibly less insistent, but often more important, considerations of policy. Thirdly, he has to tender advice to superior authority upon the manner in which existing administrative arrangements serve their purpose or the extent to which they should be altered, and to answer such particular inquiries as may be addressed to him.

Policy and legislation are, of course, laid down for the local administrator by the central government. The latter, for our present purpose, consists of two principal enactments, the Native Authority Ordinance[1] and the Native Courts Ordinance.[2] Certain other Ordinances come into the picture, to some extent, for example the Hut and Poll Tax Ordinance,[3] the Credit to Natives (Restriction) Ordinance,[4] and the Master and Native Servants Ordinance.[5] It is impracticable here to give a full list of these enactments, but references or explanations are given in the following pages, wherever they appear to be necessary.

As regards policy, it is difficult to summarize within the limits that space must impose here. Volumes have been written about the various systems of local administration, usually described by the convenient term 'indirect rule'. This principle aims at teaching the people to administer their own affairs, by adapting

[1] Cap. 47 of the Laws of Tanganyika Territory.
[2] Ordinance No. 5 of 1929, Laws of Tanganyika Territory.
[3] Cap. 63 of the Laws of Tanganyika Territory.
[4] Ordinance No. 16 of 1931, Laws of Tanganyika Territory.
[5] Cap. 51 of the Laws of Tanganyika Territory.

the institutions which they have evolved for themselves, so that they may develop in a constitutional manner from their own past, guided and restrained by their own traditions and sanctions and by the general advice and control of administrative officers.

In Tanganyika, these native institutions have been brought within the ambit of our system of indirect rule and made part of our local constitution by means of the Native Authority Ordinance,[1] under which such native political organizations as the Government decides to recognize are given legal status by being declared 'Native Authorities', with certain specified powers.

In the particular tribe in connexion with which this work has been carried out, the chief is the superior Native Authority, and, with his advisers, is the fount of all authority within the tribal unit. He has delegated some of his authority to nine sub-chiefs, each ruling over a certain well-defined area and each having been appointed to be a subordinate Native Authority subject to the Superior Authority. Each subordinate Native Authority has its own native court. The Superior Authority has a higher court and also exercises appellate jurisdiction from the courts of the Subordinate Authorities. The jurisdiction of all these courts is defined in the Native Courts Ordinance[2] and in the warrant which is issued to each court, specimens of which will be found in Appendix A. It may be

[1] Op. cit., p. 10.
[2] Op. cit., p. 10.

summarized as the power to punish breaches of native law and custom and to adjudicate upon disputes in accordance with that law and custom, to the extent that is laid down for each court in its warrant. In addition, the Native Authority Ordinance confers upon Native Authorities the power to make orders and rules for certain purposes, and when these have been lawfully made, they are within the jurisdiction of the courts of the area within which they have been made and their breach may be punished in those courts.[1]

Finally, the Native Administration has its own treasury, which pays the salaries of the Native Authorities and subordinate personnel, provides funds to build court houses, dispensaries, and schools, to make and maintain roads, and to establish various other local services, subject to such supervision as is necessary to prevent waste and misappropriation.

The revenue of the native treasury is derived from a share of the hut and poll tax (which is collected by the Native Authorities), court fees and fines, certain local fees and dues (e.g. fees for the registration of

[1] There is one exception to this. In certain circumstances orders are made by the Native Authorities at the instance, and on behalf of, the central government or its local agents. This generally takes the form of orders for the engagement of paid labour for essential public services, under section 8 (*i*) of the Native Authority Ordinance, but may occur in relation to certain other matters. In all such cases, i.e. cases in which work or service is being done or rendered at the instance, direct or indirect, of the Government or any of its officers, delinquents may not be tried by the native courts.

marriages and divorces, ferry fees, &c.), and the sale of produce from seed-farms.[1]

The Native Authorities are not, of course, independent rulers, and their powers are strictly limited to such as may be delegated to them by the Governor, whose representative is the Provincial Commissioner and, under him, the District Officer. The Government reserves to itself the right to impose taxation, to make laws, to control the exercise of such subsidiary legislative powers as may be delegated to the Native Authorities, to dispose of such lands as are vested in the paramount power 'for the use and common benefit, direct and indirect, of the natives of the Territory',[2] and, of course, to raise and control armed forces.

Further, the disposal of the annual revenue of the native treasury, the appointment and dismissal of important officers of the Native Administration, and, indeed, all the important executive acts of the Native Authority, though emanating from itself, are subject to the guidance and advice of the District Officer. The latter is not, however, the direct executive authority for native affairs in the area of administration of a Native Authority. He advises and guides and supervises, but refrains from giving direct orders unless the Native Authority fails to fulfil the functions for

[1] A skeleton budget of the Uhehe Native Treasury is given in Appendix B.
[2] Section 3 of the Land Ordinance, Cap. 68 of the Laws of Tanganyika Territory.

which it was established. Though the parallel is by no means exact, the relationship might be compared to that existing between the Ministry of Health and local government bodies in England.

The District Officer is also responsible for the supervision and control of the native courts and for scrutinizing and checking the accuracy of their records. But unless he considers that they are not carrying out satisfactorily their primary function (which is to give effect to the well-established and understood body of customary law which regulates native society) or that a miscarriage of justice has resulted from a decision they have given, he does not normally interfere with their judgements, though he has full powers of revisional jurisdiction over them.

In addition to the supervision of the Native Authorities, the administrator is, of course, responsible generally for the maintenance of good government in his district. It is his duty to provide security of person and property and to allow for the enjoyment of personal rights and the redress of wrongs, in a manner compatible with the standards of civilized government. He must preserve organized society without arresting its natural and proper development, keeping alive the spirit of social and communal responsibility, while fostering at the same time self-respect and pride of race.

An equitable system of taxation and of its collection is a first essential of good government. This involves, for the administrator, an assessment based on the economic capacity of the tax-payer to pay and the compilation of accurate assessment rolls. Methods of collection must be evolved, and constant supervision is necessary to prevent them from operating with undue harshness, while, on the other hand, ensuring that they are efficient enough to reduce to a minimum the number of wilful defaulters.

The administrator must also promote economic development within his district, as a means whereby the standard of living of the people may be raised. This necessitates co-operation with members of technical departments to introduce new economic crops and to evolve the best methods of marketing them. He must also seek their assistance in encouraging improved methods of agriculture as a means to greater crop-production, when tackling such problems as over-stocking and soil erosion, and in his efforts to combat the evils of shifting cultivation and the indiscriminate destruction of forest.

Finally, the rapid development which the native is undergoing as a result of his contact with western civilization entails a continual modification of existing administrative arrangements to meet new demands. In this, the administrator plays a leading part; and it is his duty to advise the central government on such diverse subjects as the effects of European settlement on tribal life, the sociological consequences of wage-labour, the material and social results of the introduction of new religions, the causes and effects of detribalization, and the problems surrounding education.

It will thus be seen that, to administer a tribe effectively under the conditions outlined above, the administrator should acquire a wide knowledge of many aspects of native culture. While not wishing to be dogmatic as to the extent of this knowledge, we desire briefly to indicate those fields he would find useful in practice.

In the first place, he will wish to know something of the native political organization, the status of the various tribal functionaries, and the position occupied by the subject in the tribe. He should understand the importance of the family and the part which kinship plays in tribal activities. He will also study the rules of marriage and divorce and the attitude of the tribe towards religion and the introduction of new beliefs.

While it is seldom possible for the administrator to understand the whole corpus of native law, he should at least acquire a working knowledge of its principles and procedure. It will be necessary for him to know something of the law of evidence and the consideration which is given to it in the making of judicial decisions. He will be interested to discover the sociological and political significance of any customary forms of punishment which may be practised to-day, and should study the native attitude towards our law and the effects on tribal life of our system of punishments. When dealing with a particular tribe, he will also wish to be informed on the more specific problems which will inevitably arise from time to time.

Examples of this will be discussed in the following chapters.

As the majority of African tribes obtain their living, directly or indirectly, from the land, it is necessary for the administrator to investigate the question of native land tenure in all its aspects. He will examine the system under which it is held, the law of succession regarding it, the uses to which it is put by the tribe, and their present and future requirements in this direction. The importance of the latter questions will vary with different tribes and will depend on whether they are agricultural or pastoral, on the quantity of land available in relation to population, on rainfall distribution and soil erosion, and on many other factors, too numerous to mention here.

In the economic sphere, the administrator should be in possession of a great deal of knowledge, before any attempt is made to raise the standard of living. It is necessary, first, to study the economic organization in relation to the whole social structure of the tribe, so as to ensure that any development will rest on sound foundations. This will include an examination of the customary division of labour, the extent of community co-operation, and the sources of income of the average peasant. This latter line of inquiry will in turn bring into review the question of wage-labour, and information will be sought as to the general conditions under which it is recruited, and how it travels, lives, and works.

For the proper administration of a tribe, some

knowledge, too, should be acquired regarding native custom and belief in such matters as magic and witchcraft. It will also be necessary, in the case of most Bantu tribes, to obtain details of their initiation ceremonies, in order to determine to what degree they are harmful or repugnant to our ideas of morality.

From this general description of the functions and duties of an administrator and of the knowledge he requires of native institutions to enable him to carry them out successfully, it will be realized how this knowledge must be sought from a wide variety of angles. Such questions as he may put to the anthropologist, therefore, however much they are based on the general principles outlined above, must often be asked in a disjointed manner, one question having little relation to that which precedes or that which follows it. In short, to be useful they must arise from the exigencies of the moment.

In this experiment, the earlier questions were, in fact, asked in such an apparently unsystematic way; each one was asked within the limits laid down, but no attempt was made to arrange them in any order. After a period of about eight months, however, it became desirable and practicable to group and classify them in accordance with some definite principle. Two methods of classification were possible. One was to group the questions in terms of their relevance to the problems of administration. This was tried and ultimately rejected, because it did not seem that it would result in a clear understanding of the facts presented. The other method was to arrange the questions in terms of their relation to an easily understood analysis of the basis of tribal life. This principle was finally adopted, and made possible an orderly treatment of those aspects of Hehe culture which were considered important to the main aim of the experiment.[1]

Thus the system of question and answer resulted in emphasizing the importance of certain fields of knowledge and in minimizing certain others. The presentation of the results which follows is an attempt to organize the relevant knowledge in accordance with the guidance so given. Various omissions will surprise anthropologists, and an attempt will be made to explain these omissions in the course of the presentation; the emphasis laid on certain points may be equally surprising; but in every case, omission or emphasis is determined by a careful consideration of relation to the agreed practical end.

[1] A list of the questions asked during the course of the experiment and specimen answers to three of them will be found in Appendix C.

II
THE HEHE TRIBE

THE content of this account of the Hehe tribe is determined, as explained in the previous chapter, by administrative needs. This consideration limits the material and imposes the obligation of describing tribal life primarily as it exists to-day; a description of the tribe as it existed before European occupation can only be justified by the light it throws on present-day social and political problems. Thus an account of the old political organization is given, but only to show the materials out of which the present political structure is being created. Similarly the old law of inheriting wives is explained, but only to illustrate the process of change which is occurring in marital relationships.[1]

Once the principle is accepted that the emphasis is to be laid on the present, certain conclusions follow as a matter of course. It is, for example, essential for the administrator to have some fairly definite criteria by which to determine what constitutes native law and custom. Most African tribes have been administered for at least one generation; many for several generations. Is native law and custom to be taken as

---

[1] This emphasis on the present social structure is, we hope, fully justified by practical considerations. We also believe it theoretically justifiable; but a discussion on that point is beyond the limits of this monograph.

that which existed before continuous contact with Europeans? Or are changes which have occurred under foreign administrative, religious, and economic influences to be taken as constituting an integral part of native custom? The adoption of our simple principle forces us to the latter point of view. Hehe law and custom are taken here simply to mean the sum total of those observances as recognized by the tribe at the present day. Thus, before European occupation, the widows of a dead man must be inherited by one of certain heirs, usually a brother of the deceased. As a result of European occupation, it has become accepted that no woman need be inherited against her will. Nowadays, a woman may be inherited, but if she objects, she goes to the native courts and is automatically given a divorce. According to the point of view taken in this account, the present practice is the native law. The same thing applies when some new element is introduced. Before European occupation, the bodies of dead commoners were not buried, but were thrown into the bush. The German administrators ordered that all corpses were to be buried. A new set of observances arose to meet this new enactment. Deaths must now be reported to the headman; he views the body, gives orders for burial, and details a number of men to dig the grave. These new observances are taken to be as much a part of Hehe custom and law as those which existed before burial became universal. In brief, Hehe law and custom is the totality of those social observances which are accepted as normal by the majority of the tribesmen and which can be enforced by the tribal organization.

A distinction must be made between new customs accepted by the tribe and new laws and orders affecting the tribe. Under the Penal Code, for example, murderers must be dealt with in a certain way, and executed if convicted. This can hardly be called native custom, because the murderer is apprehended by the police and tried by a European judge. Similarly, a new tribal order restricts the cutting of trees, to preserve the forests.[1] Offences against this order are tried by the native courts, but it is only by virtue of the authority of the administrative and forest officers that the order is observed. The native administration may co-operate to secure the observance of the new legal code or of administrative orders; but they are not native custom because they are not accepted by the tribe as part of their own code of behaviour, and because their own social organization cannot, by itself, enforce observance. An administrative order or a new law may in time be absorbed into the body of native law and custom, but at any given time it is fairly easy for one who knows a tribe to determine what new factors have been so absorbed and what have not.

[1] Order made by the Chief under Section 8 (*f*) of the Native Authority Ordinance, op. cit., p. 12.

A. *SOCIAL ORGANIZATION*

1. POLITICAL ORGANIZATION

Early in the experiment, the anthropologist was asked to give a full account of the political organization of the tribe. This request was supplemented later by more specific questions: these were either requests for immediate information, or indications of the necessity for expansion on certain points. The following pages should therefore offer little conflict with accepted notions as to what constitutes a full description of political organization; for it is an attempt at as complete and clear an account of Hehe political life as is compatible with brevity, dwelling a little more on some points than would ordinarily be expected, but with no excessive emphasis.

(*a*) *The Tribe*.

The people nowadays called Hehe are really a political entity of recent growth. Up to the eighteen-fifties, the units now constituting the tribe were a number of small tribes, probably similar in speech and custom, but with no political unity. It is impossible to state exactly how many of these small units there were, but we have discovered the existence of twenty-nine,[1] and it is possible that some of these included two or three independent political groups.

A knowledge of the pre-existence of these small tribes is useful for two reasons. First, they have a

[1] A list of them is given in Appendix D.

minor political importance to-day. All the people of the tribe will, after first announcing that they are Hehe, tell one that their real tribe is so-and-so, naming the original tribe to which they belonged. The term Hehe is applied to the whole group, it is not the name of a tribe that conquered all the rest. The importance of this point will be dealt with in connexion with the present sub-chiefs. The second, more significant, fact is that they were welded together by two able men, Muyugumba, the grandfather, and Mkwawa, the father of the present chief; and the tales told of the progress of conquest constitute the charter both of the tribe and of the right of the Muyinga family to rule. The existence of the tribe as a tribe is thus intimately related to the rising fortunes of the present ruling family. It is, therefore, convenient to begin an account of the tribe by giving the story of the chiefly family; not because this story necessarily gives a true history of events, but because it is told and believed throughout the tribe. Moreover, it is considered a sufficient account of the origin of the tribe and the paramountcy of the Muyinga family.

The story begins with Mufwimi, son of a chief, who came from Usagara on a hunting trip, accompanied by his brother. The brothers quarrelled, and Mufwimi, after a long chase, found himself in Nguruhe, where he was hospitably received by the local chief, Mududa. He stayed some time and became the lover of the chief's daughter. She became pregnant, and he, fearing the anger of her father, ran away. Before he left, he told her what to name the child; he told her his clan, praise-name, and avoidances. A son was born, was named Muyinga, was given the praise-name Mulugu, and was told to avoid eating the *funo* (small buck), the *nyakihuko* (large rat), and food cooked by a certain kind of wood[1]—all according to his father's instructions. The ruling family have these names and avoidances at the present day, and, as a clan, call themselves the Va-Muyinga. The story goes on to tell how the young Muyinga circumvented the plots of his maternal uncles and how he finally, on the death of his maternal grandfather, drove out his uncles and inherited the chieftainate. The story then becomes genealogical: Muyinga was succeeded by his son Maduga, and the succession continued by unbroken descent from father to son through Maliga, Mudegela, to Kilonge. Kilonge was succeeded by Ngawanalupembe; the latter died after a year and was succeeded by his brother Muyugumba. With the succession of Muyugumba begins the creation of the Hehe tribe, and the story begins to approximate more closely to verifiable history.

Muyugumba seems to have peacefully added to his lands shortly after his accession, and this probably made him more powerful than any of the other petty chiefs; so that, whether deliberately or not, he embarked on a career of conquest. The stories of his various wars become tedious. At his death, which probably occurred in 1879, he had conquered at least

[1] See below, p. 84.

all the peoples now called Hehe, and had waged war with the Sangu and with the more powerful Ngoni.

His eldest son, Mkwawa, was driven out by a hostile faction when Muyugumba died, and went to the Gogo country. He was brought back after two years, established his authority, and followed his father's warlike example. The stories of Mkwawa's reign are much the same as those of his father's: reconquest of the Hehe tribes, wars with more powerful enemies, and the general consolidation of the tribe as a whole. His reign and life were terminated by the German conquest. This brief indication of the outline of the tribal legends is sufficient for the present purpose.

The Hehe were formed into a political unit by conquest, but became a genuinely united tribe by the growth of various sanctions and the development of complex political institutions. But though there was a large group considering itself Hehe, it is almost impossible to determine the exact limits of that group, to decide who became genuine Hehe, who remained mere conquered communities, and who merely acknowledged some sort of hegemony.

Allowing for some exceptions, it seems probable that when the tribal authority was reconstituted in 1926 the boundaries were extremely well chosen, and that the present Iringa District indicates fairly well the area populated by genuine Hehe. To the east and south-east, the escarpment makes a natural boundary, and there is no suggestion that the people below the escarpment were ever fully absorbed. The people above the escarpment, the Tsungwa, although they show slight variations in language and custom from the central Hehe and although they distinguish themselves from their conquerors, nevertheless seem to identify themselves politically with the Muyinga family and to have become Hehe. To the south, the boundary is roughly indicated by the Bena country; the Bena were always the conquered and never became identified with their conquerors. The boundary would have been difficult to fix exactly, and the one chosen was as good as any other. To the west, the Sangu were always a separate group; and, while there is much evidence that a large part of their country was conquered and more of it periodically raided, there was never any effective absorption. To the north-east, below the escarpment but south of the Ruaha, the people speak of themselves as Sagala (Sagara), but the Muyinga family themselves are Sagala, and there seems no doubt that they were politically absorbed. To the north only is the matter of the boundary in doubt. The people between the escarpment and the Ruaha are a mixture of many fragments of tribes; they were conquered, frequently raided, but never absorbed. The central Hehe refer to them, with some contempt, as 'Gogo', but they could probably be included as well with the Hehe as with any other larger unit. The influence of the Hehe extended farther north, well into the Gogo country; and they seem to have established ruling colonies among the Gogo people, as well as among the Bena and the

Sangu; but the recurrence of raids in these three countries, up to a short time before the German occupation, proves that there was never any effective conquest.

Probably the general situation may be summed up by saying that the people in the central part of the tribe became Hehe, that is, they considered themselves primarily subjects of the Muyinga rulers. Towards the borders of the present Iringa District, this loyalty lessened, and periodic raids or expeditions were necessary to reinforce the authority of the tribal rulers. Beyond the present District, the superiority of the Hehe was generally allowed, but no absorption took place; the people either peacefully acquiesced in conquest, or were periodically in revolt and had to be reconquered. This conclusion might be illustrated in further detail, but for the present purpose the broad facts are sufficient.

(b) *The Chief*.

The political organization evolved was continuously changing, and there is no reason for considering one period superior to another. The institutions of the tribe which are here taken as the normal are those which existed in the years of Mkwawa's reign, just before the first German expedition in 1891. The principal reason for describing this period is that the facts are relatively easy to obtain. Many men now living were adults in that period, and general statements are derived from a large number of concrete facts, recounted by eyewitnesses. There is also a theoretical justification for choosing this period. Hehe political organization then attained a unity that it never had before and has hardly had since; and, in the memories of the men who experienced that unity, it forms a standard by which political organization may be judged.

As stated, the nucleus of this unity was the chieftainate; and an account of the functions of the chief makes a convenient beginning for a description of the whole tribal organization. The chief was and is called *mutwa*. This term implies paramountcy and all the functions associated with the exercise of the chiefly power. As in the case of most African chiefs, the powers of the chief of the Hehe were indivisible: he was judge, maker and guardian of the law, the repository of wealth, dispenser of gifts, and leader in war—in European parlance, his functions were judicial, legislative, administrative, economic, and military. We shall find this same indivisibility of function throughout the whole tribal hierarchy: no matter how subordinate a sub-chief or headman, he had, within the community assigned to him, the same undivided powers.

The chief was regarded primarily as judge. As will be explained later, he was both interpreter of the law and keeper of the peace. Appeals could be made to him, and serious offences such as murder, treason, or witchcraft could only be judged by him. To assist him in his judicial capacity, he had a council of *vatambuli*, that is of men he had called (*ku-tambula*, to call, name, or designate) to his capital for that purpose. These men were chosen, partly from reasons of friendship, but chiefly on account of their skill in sifting evidence and in interpreting the law. They were not necessarily, nor even usually, old men, but generally men in the prime of life whose legal ability had obtained general social recognition.[1] In general, these men probably decided the majority of cases brought to the chief. Only in more serious cases, or when he was particularly interested, would the chief do more than confirm their decisions.

As final judge, the chief almost inevitably had legislative powers. Case-law, the mode in which general principles are interpreted in special instances, can change primitive as much as it can civilized law. But the chief also legislated directly. At large gatherings, he made new decrees, and these must be accepted by all his sub-chiefs in their administrative or judicial capacities. We have not been able to determine the exact nature of these decrees. It is certain that they did not greatly alter the social structure; and it seems probable that they were what might be classified as administrative decrees, and that they referred chiefly to the tribal military levy, to taxation, to emergency measures for dealing with such matters as famine, or to measures concerned with the maintenance or increase of the chief's prerogatives. There is plenty of

[1] Hence the insistence nowadays that the native courts have old men to assist them would be neither particularly desirable among the Hehe nor in accordance with native custom.

evidence that such decrees were obeyed; this will be illustrated in discussing other aspects of the chief's powers.

The wealth of the chief was principally dependent upon four sources. In the first place, he owned large herds of cattle. This at once placed him above his subjects, in a tribe where wealth is counted in live-stock. This wealth was constantly renewed. The frequent forays of the tribe resulted in the acquisition of new stock; and the chief disposed of it, dividing a portion of the captured animals among those who had distinguished themselves, but keeping a generous portion for himself. He was also constantly enriched by confiscations. It was dangerous for a man to possess wealth of any sort to a degree beyond that justified by his station; he was fortunate if he escaped with his life and the loss of most of his cattle. Finally, in a sense the chief regarded all cattle as his to dispose of. In war-time, for instance, each subordinate leader must take cattle to the field to feed the fighting men; and even in peace-time, requisitions of cattle were not rare.

The second source of wealth was forced labour. Any man could be ordered to build a house for the chief or any member of his family, and the house so built must be better than those of commoners. The largest communal effort of which we have any record was the building of the wall around Kalenga, the chief's capital. This was begun in the latter part of the eighteen-eighties and was finished in 1891. It enclosed a space of more than a square mile. It was about 8 feet high, built of two lines of stakes between which mud and stones were packed, and had fourteen doors, each one placed in a bay, so that the approach could be covered by musketry fire. A large number of men worked at it during the dry seasons of several years, and some men, brought from a long distance, worked the whole year round.

A third source of wealth was organized tribute. Every headman was responsible for the cultivation of a garden by communal labour, the produce of which was to go to the chief. In practice, we are told, this was generally neglected; so that at the harvest time the headman had to make a levy on all the members of his community, to supply the necessary tribute for the chief.

A fourth source of wealth was the monopoly of the ivory trade. All elephant-hunters were supplied with guns and ammunition by the chief; the tusks were brought to him, and, at least once a year, convoys were sent to Kilosa or to Bagamoyo to exchange them for guns, ammunition, cloth, and smaller articles such as beads and ornamental brass nails. These goods were distributed to the tribe. Each man got cloth from the chief for his own use and for his wives, in accordance with his rank and his reputation as a warrior; and the guns and ammunition were given to selected leaders and warriors. This organized generosity was responsible for binding the members of the tribe to their chief.

It is, of course, the use of wealth, not its accumulation, that is the important aspect of primitive political power. The co-ordinating influence of the distribution of trade goods is obvious. Accumulated stocks of grain and of large herds of cattle were used for a similar purpose. They formed emergency stores in case of famine, allowed judicious presents to be made to reward useful services, and fed the warriors in time of war. The chief was thus looked upon as the source of wealth, of reward, and of sustenance in times of trouble; and his power was strengthened accordingly.

The chief was also the leader in war. This was an important function among the Hehe, and perhaps it is the function that is best remembered to-day. As previously noted, the Hehe tribe was created by conquest. For many years there were annual expeditions. In the time of Muyugumba, the founder of the tribe (1855–79), the military function was the principal one. As each conquered community became successively absorbed, it supplied, in its turn, warriors to extend the conquests. Universal service for all able-bodied men became the rule. Thus military service became an instrument of tribal integration, not because it created an army for keeping the Hehe communities subject, but because it drew all the men together to strive for a common object, under a common head. Service, and therefore obedience, to the chief thus reinforced the other tribal bonds.

Each chief strengthened his position by the collection of medicine. He did not acquire it in the same manner as a magician, but collected special medicines to promote his power. Thus Mkwawa had various medicines for giving his men before battle; medicines for placating or driving away his enemies; and medicines to protect himself, his family, and his adherents against the many dangers which surround a man raised above his fellows. To these was ascribed his success against his opponents, when he returned to the tribe after being driven out; and medicine equally received the credit for his successes against his enemies.

There were still other sanctions to the rule of the chief and thus to tribal unity. Religion became an integrating factor. The effective religion of the Hehe is ancestor-worship.[1] Each man sacrifices to and supplicates his own ancestors upon certain occasions. The only tribal deities, who can be called upon for aid in emergencies affecting the whole tribe, are the souls of people who have been rulers over the whole land. These can only be invoked through the medium of the chief himself: he prays for their aid in time of drought and for help in war. The chief was thus, in a very limited but nevertheless effective sense, the chief priest of the tribe. He increased the strength of this sanction by forbidding his sub-chiefs and headmen to pray for rain, except with his express permission or by his order.

The ceremonial privileges of the chief increased his consequence in the eyes of his subjects. He was surrounded by a vast household. He had many wives,

[1] See below, section E of this chapter, pp. 166–172.

both at his own residence and at other places of importance throughout the tribe. He also had slaves to attend him. Slaves were of two types: war prisoners, such as were possessed by a large number of Hehe; and a particular group of slaves, devoted to the chief alone, the *vafugwa*. The latter were a distinct class, who inherited their status patrilineally. Their functions were two: to tend the chief's donkeys, which was considered an unclean task, and to supply children to be buried with the chiefs and their children when they died. They were despised, so much so that to call a man a *mufugwa* was and still is slander, even if true. The chief defended them against the rest of the tribe and they were completely dependent upon him.

A crowd of other adherents were also around him. The *vanya mulyango*, 'those who stand by the door', were his guards and his messengers. He also had an 'announcer', a man with a loud and penetrating voice, to proclaim his laws and his orders. One of the more interesting groups he collected around him were the *vigendo*, 'those who go'. These were young boys, from about the ages of twelve to twenty, who formed a sort of corps of attendants. They were either chosen by the chief or sent by their fathers. There is some evidence that a certain amount of instruction was given them and that they were sometimes taken away from the chief's residence for that purpose by their instructors, but their chief functions seem to have been to form a retinue for the chief and to bind the various parts of the tribe to him, by assembling children from all areas for his service. When they grew up, the chief assisted them to procure wives. They passed out in groups, each with its own name, and they lived together in groups afterwards. Under Muyugumba, they were planted out as military colonies among newly conquered peoples. Mkwawa kept them near him, settling them in groups in his capital at Kalenga.

Besides the special adherents of his court, Mkwawa ordered two or three thousand men to live in his capital. This had to be done by order, because the Hehe prefer living in scattered settlements. They were thus permanently assembled to act as a guard for himself, and they could be quickly assembled for battle in an emergency.

Other prerogatives of the chief might be classified as sumptuary and ceremonial. He alone could sit on a stool decorated with brass nails. He, and those who paid him for the privilege only, could exact a high bride-wealth (*mafungu*) on the marriage of their daughters.[1] He, and the descendants of paramount chiefs only, had the right to be buried; and finally, he was greeted by a special salutation *atse senga*, a courtesy only extended to those descendants of paramount chiefs who were in actual possession of political power.

These were the constituent factors of the chieftainate when it came to an end in 1898: a combination of

[1] Cf. G. Gordon Brown, 'Bride-wealth among the Hehe', *Africa*, vol. v, no. 2, pp. 145–57.

powers, privileges, and obligations which succeeded in making a tribe of a large number of smaller tribal units. It is futile to speculate whether this tribal unity would have continued had there been no European conquest; the purely native development was interrupted, and, for nearly thirty years, the chieftainate was in abeyance.

After the suicide of Mkwawa, the Germans made efforts to rule through one of his brothers. This arrangement did not work satisfactorily, and for various reasons five of them were hanged. The chief's children were sent to schools, Sapi, the heir to the chieftainate, being educated at Dar es Salaam and later in Germany. During the whole period of the German occupation the chief concern of the administration was the maintenance of law and order; the greater sub-chiefs had their powers gradually reduced; and, at the outbreak of the War, the German administration was ruling directly through the local headmen; tribal unity was, for the time, destroyed.

The British officials took over the native organization much as the Germans had left it, and they continued to utilize the headmen as instruments of administration until 1926. In that year the principle known as indirect rule was extended to the Hehe, and it became necessary to restore the tribal organization.

The officials whose task it was to create some organization through which the whole tribe was to be administered had two alternatives. They could either recognize the effective power developed by the headmen during the generation that had elapsed since a chief had ruled, and attempt to form them into a unified governing group; or they could restore the chieftainate. The latter alternative was adopted, wisely in our opinion, since tribal unity was associated with the chief and with the ruling family. Once the principle was decided upon, the choice of the person was inevitable. The Hehe rule is that the eldest son of the chief wife, that is the first wife, succeeds his father to office. This rule is sometimes relaxed when the rightful heir is incapable; and also, sometimes, when the son of another wife is older than the rightful heir, he manages to obtain the succession. In choosing the Hehe chief, there was no possibility of ambiguity. Sapi was the eldest son of Mkwawa and child of his first wife. The assembled headmen and elders informed the District Officer that if a chief were to be chosen, it must be Sapi. He was accordingly installed as chief in 1926.[1]

A Hehe chief, ruling under the supervision of an administrative officer, is obviously in a very different position from an independent paramount chief. It may be useful to suggest the resemblances and the differences, so that some judgement may be formed of the extent to which the old tribal organization has

[1] In 1920 Sapi had returned to the tribe and resumed the chieftainate. Matters were not well managed, however, and much trouble arose. The result was that he was removed from office within a few months.

been restored and the extent to which a new organization has been created.

In the first place, there is no doubt that the tribe accept the chief as the only man who has the right to the office. His family is the symbol of tribal unity. It is still a privilege to belong to his, the Muyinga, clan and to be addressed by the praise-name of his clan, Mulugu.[1] Moreover, the past greatness of the tribe is associated with the Muyinga family. As already explained, the history and the legends that have grown up around the exploits of the ancestors of the present chief mean much to the Hehe. They are the charter of the paramount rights of the ruling family, of tribal unity, and of superiority to other tribes. The Hehe have no myths: to explain the origin of the tribe, they consider it sufficient to give the stories of the ruling families and, in particular, the stories associated with the Muyinga family.

The existence of this body of legend and traditional history makes it possible to re-create the power of the chieftainate. But it is definitely a re-creation, not a restoration, with many changes in the functions of the chief. As judge, his position is in many ways similar to that of his predecessors. He interprets the body of customary law, hears appeals from the judgements of his sub-chiefs, and generally exercises a considerable influence upon the growth and administration of

[1] Cf. also G. Gordon Brown, 'Legitimacy and Paternity among the Hehe', *American Journal of Sociology*, vol. xxxviii, no. 2, Sept. 1932.

Hehe law. On the other hand, his powers are curtailed. Under the Native Courts Ordinance,[1] his jurisdiction is limited to the hearing of cases in which both parties are natives resident within the tribal area. In civil suits, he may not try cases in which the subject-matter exceeds £30 in value. For criminal offences, he may not inflict sentences of imprisonment exceeding six months, of fine exceeding £10, or of whipping of more than eight strokes.[2] He can, of course, always order the payment of appropriate compensation, in addition to or in lieu of the sentences detailed above. All his judgements are subject to appeal to the District Officer, and, finally, all serious crime is dealt with by a European magistrate. With all these limitations, however, his function as judge has changed less than any other, and he is still possessed of a wide range of judicial power.

It is as administrator that the change is greater, and a new analysis of his administrative duties is necessary. These duties may be divided into police, financial, and general executive duties. Of his police duties, little need be said except that he is able to call upon all officials of the native administration, with their intimate knowledge of the kinship relations of the people, to assist in the capture of criminals. He is thus able to render police services which regular policemen cannot. He is responsible for the general peace and good government of his tribe. This is mostly accom-

---

[1] Op. cit., p. 10.
[2] See below, Appendix A, pp. 241–2.

plished through his function as judge, but he must and does co-operate with the District Officer to bring criminals to justice and to prevent crime.

The financial duties, of course, have all been imposed as a result of European occupation. They consist in the collection of the hut and poll tax and of fines and fees and local dues, and the disbursement of the tribal revenue.[1] These duties have a considerable effect upon the tribal concept of the present-day chieftainate.

In the first place, the collection of tax by the chief and his subordinates identifies him with the Government, and so supports his authority. A new sanction is thus added to the sanctions of the olden days. This sanction, of course, would not be effective by itself: a chief would not be accepted merely because he was supported by the Government; but it does strengthen the other sanctions. It will be noted later that the function of tax-collection similarly strengthens the position of the other officials in the political hierarchy.

In the second place, the fact that he can employ so many men (clerks, messengers, and other tribal functionaries) gives him an influence which resembles, in a very attenuated manner, the power his father concentrated in himself by strengthening the loyalty of his followers through the distribution of cloth. But this power is both attenuated and divided. It is well known that the District Officer has at least as much

[1] See above, p. 12.

to say about the employment of tribal servants as the chief has. All that can be stated is that the association of the chief with governmental functions acts as a prop to his authority.

Considering the chief as a financial agent of Government, there is little to say. There is no suggestion that he abuses his financial powers. Corruption there is, but it will be shown that it comes lower in the tribal hierarchy. Taxes are collected impartially as far as the chief is concerned, and disbursements are made with equal honesty.

The chief still enjoys some privileges that do not come strictly within the letter of the law. His gardens are cultivated by communal labour—this can hardly be called forced labour, since the service seems to be rendered willingly. Similarly, he gets free service from his subjects when he is building or repairing his houses. In no case does the burden fall heavily on any one person, and the people do not appear to resent these small exactions: they are all taken as among the privileges of chieftainship.

There exist also privileges that are recognized even though there is no direct attempt to enforce them. Whenever the chief travels, he and his followers are supplied with free food; and, in addition, each headman through whose area he passes is expected to present him with an ox. All these privileges are small and they perform a useful function: that of emphasizing the fact of his chieftainate, and consequently making his authority more effective. If any of them were unduly enforced, they would become serious abuses. As they are recognized by the tribe to-day, they are no more than complimentary recognitions of his position.

The Hehe thus accept the chief both as the hereditary ruler of the tribe and as the chief recognized by the Government; both sanctions are necessary to his effective power.

It would give a false picture of conditions to suggest that the chief is universally accepted and approved. There is a small minority which dislikes him. There are, first, the headmen, whose power was curtailed by his restoration. Not all of them nor even the majority of them are hostile to him, but a number of them resent his presence; and they were instrumental in having him removed after his brief period of restoration in 1920. This opposition is decreasing as the nature of the new order is recognized. Secondly, there are a group of sophisticated[1] natives who object to his authority, but these are small in number. Thirdly, there are a few adherents of the representative of a collateral branch of the Muyinga family, who claim this person as the rightful heir;[2] but they are

[1] By 'sophisticated' is not meant 'well educated', but the group of people living in towns who have a superficial acquaintance with the trappings of European culture and government and who have an ignoble contempt for the 'primitive' natives living the tribal life.
[2] On an obscure point of the law of succession. The validity of the point at issue is doubtful, and as it extends back for three generations it is not worth discussion.

few and unorganized. There are, fourthly, a small number of unorganized tribal conservatives, who adhere to the tribal ruler as the family representative, but who feel that his absence of more than twenty years from the tribe and his education at the coast and in Germany have made his outlook too foreign for a tribal chief. Finally, there are a number of people who dislike him on various personal grounds. It is, for example, made a matter of complaint that he is too apt to promote the interests of members of his own family, at the expense of others. No one of these groups is really organized, however, and their existence does little to impair the effective exercise of his authority.

(c) *The Sub-chiefs*.

The central authority established by Muyugumba and Mkwawa did not depend solely upon the powers of the chiefs themselves. They instituted a judicious system of delegation and of subordination, from which, with a good many changes, have developed the sub-chiefs and the headmen of the present day.

To understand the system of delegation of power, it is necessary to bear in mind the manner in which the Hehe tribe was created. A number of independent tribes were made subordinate to one chief. As these tribes submitted or were conquered, the ruling families were dealt with in various ways. Generally they were retained and made subordinate chiefs. Sometimes the conquered chief was given his whole country back again, sometimes a part of it. In other cases, the ruling chief was driven out and the country given to a younger brother, or to some collateral branch of the family. In still other cases, an entirely new ruler was chosen. In addition to these, appointees of the paramount chief were given posts throughout the tribe. These nominees were sometimes brothers of the chief. Mkwawa gave several of his brothers subordinate power: Mpangile at Igominyi, near Wasa; and Kong'oke, a son of his father's brother,[1] at Malangali. Still other appointees were sons-in-law of the chief. The most important person in the tribe under Mkwawa was his brother-in-law Ngotsingotsi (son-in-law of Muyugumba): this man was equivalent to the commander-in-chief of the army and prime minister. Friends or distant relatives of the chief were also appointed sub-chiefs and were given territories where local chiefs were expected to give trouble. In so far as one can interpret his policy, Mkwawa seems to have aimed at keeping local chiefs when it was possible to do so, and at balancing their power by these new appointments.

These subordinate chiefs, or sub-chiefs as they are now called, were given different titles, according to their status. A brother of the chief was called *mutwa* as was the chief. A son-in-law was called *mwanamtwa* (literally, child of a chief). The general term, however, for denoting the possessor of a delegated or subordinate power is *muntsagila*; and even a man called

[1] And thus a brother; see below, p. 91.

mutwa or *mwanamtwa* might be so designated, if his subordinate position was being emphasized. Thus a descendant of an old paramount chief, who was still ruling his ancestors' territories as a subordinate of the chief, would be called *mutwa* by his people, but *muntsagila* in the presence of the chief.

Of these subordinate rulers, some enjoyed more power than others, but there does not seem to have been an organized territorial hierarchy as there is to-day. Thus Mpangile at Igominyi sometimes altered the judicial decisions of the lesser sub-chiefs near him; but appeals were made to him, not in virtue of an extended territorial authority, but simply because he was more powerful than his neighbours. There seems to have been no grading of the sub-chiefs, and there was no recognized system of subordination, except subordination to the paramount chief.

The number of these sub-chiefs is difficult to estimate. Possibly there were about thirty of them. This nearly coincides with the number of small tribes constituting the Hehe tribe as a whole; and it seems probable that the divisions of the country were left much as they had been; but we have not sufficient knowledge to be certain on this point.

The sub-chiefs possessed undivided powers just as the chief did. Each was judge, leader of the local levy in war, and the possessor of wealth and general authority in his area—all these powers being subject to the overriding authority of the chief. As judge, he heard most of the cases and settled a large number of them, sending on the few cases which could not be settled by him to the chief. His judgements were subject to appeal, but the right of appeal does not seem to have been used extensively. In the matter of legal jurisdiction, it is probable that there was no exact rule. Such limited information as we have seems to show that distance played a part. The sub-chiefs living near the chief were somewhat overshadowed by his authority and appeals were relatively frequent; the farther away a sub-chief was, the more judicial power he could assume and the more his general authority approximated to that of a paramount chief. In his judicial capacity, the sub-chief, like the chief, was assisted by a selected group of advisers, the *vatambuli*, whose advice was seldom disregarded. With due allowance for the fact that he was subordinate, that certain cases were reserved for the chief, and that the general procedure probably more nearly approximated to the democracy of the small local courts,[1] he exercised his judicial functions in much the same way as the chief.

The other functions of the old sub-chiefs need no explanation. As leaders in war, they had to bring their levies to the general assembly. They had to carry out the orders of the chief, particularly to collect the grain tribute, and generally to maintain order. In addition to their duties, they enjoyed certain privileges. They were allowed to accumulate wealth in live stock. Commoners were jealously watched to see

[1] See below, section A 1 (*d*) of this chapter, pp. 66–69.

that the wealth of any one of them did not exceed his position; sub-chiefs were allowed wealth in accordance with their station. They were not only permitted, but assisted to acquire it. The annual raids on neighbouring tribes brought a regular harvest of cattle; these were divided among those who had distinguished themselves, but the sub-chiefs received a generous share. Some of these were hardly their own property, since, in a future raid, they would have to take cattle along to feed their followers; but it made them the dispensers of wealth in the same way as the chief, though to a less degree. In the annual distribution of cloth, they were also favoured and were frequently left to distribute the share assigned to their followers.

Other privileges were allowed them. They had followers similar to those of the chief. Besides the *vatambuli*, they had *vigendo* and *vanya mulyango*,[1] the following of each sub-chief being proportioned to the esteem in which he was held. And most of them had the right to be buried at death, a privilege closely associated with rank.

Under each sub-chief, or each sub-chief with territorial authority, there were a number of petty headmen called *vapakasi*. They were, on a very small scale, the replicas of the sub-chiefs. They judged petty disputes, kept the peace in their areas, and were responsible to their superiors for carrying out orders. Unlike the sub-chiefs, they seem to have had no special

[1] See above, p. 35.

privileges. Their functions will be better understood when we come to a description of the functions of their modern representatives, the *vakalani*.[1]

This was the position when the tribal organization was broken up in 1898. From 1898 until 1926, the political organization lacked a head, and during all that time the tribe was ruled directly. This meant, in effect, that it was ruled by the headmen.

It has already been noted that an attempt was made to install a brother of the chief as ruler of the tribe, and that this attempt failed. The administration next divided the tribe among a few of the greater sub-chiefs, but this also did not work. So that, within ten years of the conquest, there were actually a large number of petty rulers, none of whom possessed authority over any large area. This resulted in a re-adjustment of status. The greater sub-chiefs became headmen of smaller areas, and some of the petty headmen began to approach the status of the former sub-chiefs; thus, instead of some thirty sub-chiefs, there came into existence a much larger number of undifferentiated headmen, who were called by the old term *vantsagila* by the Hehe, and by the Germans the Swahili term *jumbes*. These *jumbes* were the really effective rulers for a generation.

During the period of their ascendancy, the *jumbes* increased their power considerably. They were the only judges, and there was no appeal to a higher court. This statement sounds unfair to the German

[1] See below, pp. 71–8.

administrators, but it is not intended to be so. The District court was open to appeal to at any time. A large number of cases were actually taken there; but, in relation to the amount of litigation which goes on in the tribe, the number of such appeals was small. The Hehe distrusted the European courts. Their judgements, based on an alien concept of justice, seemed to them capricious. The result was that the Hehe were ready to suffer an injustice they understood, rather than to seek an impartial justice which they did not understand. Some of the headmen, realizing the improbability of appeals being made, grew corrupt; and their corruption was only checked by the fear of losing subjects; for the Hehe have always retained the privilege of leaving a headman they do not like and placing themselves under another.

It was not only judicially that corruption became widespread in some headmen's areas. The introduction of a money tax helped. The German administrators were faced with the problem of building up a financial administration in an utterly primitive tribe; there were no assessment rolls, and at first no tax receipts were issued. The chance was too good to miss, and many of the headmen grew wealthy. They were not only able to embezzle large sums with safety, but did a thriving trade in the sale of tax exemptions. As the German administration grew more efficient, the chances of embezzlement were reduced; but other perquisites of the headmen remained untouched; and, although they have been still more reduced in the last few years, a few of them remain to this day.

When the chief was restored temporarily in 1920 and permanently in 1926, he was thus faced with opposition on the part of a good many of the headmen, who were jealous of their position. An astonishingly large proportion, however, supported him. The resisters, aided by circumstances, were too much for him in 1920. Since 1926, the irreconcilables have been removed and the rest have submitted, some willingly and a few from force of circumstances.

The political system established in 1926 was intended to be based on the old organization. It resembles it in certain respects, but it also has many new features. The present ranks are chief, sub-chief, headman (*jumbe*), and petty headman (*mkalani*). The sub-chiefs inherit the title (*muntsagila*) and much of the authority of the old sub-chiefs, but are not identical in status or function.

It has been indicated how, during the last generation, the old sub-chiefs became identified with the greater headmen. Had those who re-established the tribal organization wished to be antiquarian, they could have recognized those territorial offices existing before the conquest, raised the present holders above their fellows, and established roughly thirty sub-chiefs. What actually happened was that the headmen were taken as they were (with a few minor adjustments), and their position was recognized by the payment of regular salaries from the tribal treasury. The tribal territory was then divided into a number of units, each containing several headmen, and over these units were placed the new sub-chiefs. There were at first four of them, but the number has now been increased by sub-division to nine.[1] Thus the headmen and the new sub-chiefs divided the honours associated with the old sub-chiefs, and each is in a sense a new institution: the headmen by a process of growth, the sub-chiefs by deliberate creation.

The new system of delegation is different, first because of the precise dividing lines drawn between sub-chief, headman, and petty headman. The sub-chiefs have certain powers, for instance power to enforce their judgements. The headmen actually hear and decide more cases than most of the sub-chiefs, but they have no power to enforce their decisions. The headmen are distinguished from the petty headmen, in turn, by a specific recognition of their status and by the payment of a regular salary. This precise differentiation, both of rank and of function, was not made in the olden days. Then, every person of rank had his degree of consequence; some had very little, but, such as it was, it implied an undivided power, graded indeed, but roughly the same throughout the scale. Secondly, the new sub-chiefs rule over a much greater territory than the old *vantsagila*. This has its administrative justification. It is one of the aims of indirect rule to improve the standard of honesty of native justice by constant supervision. It would be impos-

---

[1] A tenth is to be established shortly.

sible to supervise thirty sub-chiefs' courts. Had administrative exigencies permitted, the re-establishment of a much greater number of sub-chiefs would have been advantageous. It would have crystallized local loyalties, and the larger number of courts would have proved convenient to those living in the more remote areas. As it is, the sub-chiefs' courts are frequently resorted to, but the settlement of disputes is still left very much to the arbitration of the headmen.

Native custom was followed in the choice of sub-chiefs. One sub-chief is the chief's brother; another his son-in-law; five are local territorial rulers or sons of old *vantsagila*; and one is a Hehe ruling an outlying group. The ninth is in a special position as sub-chief of the mixed population of Iringa township.

Sub-chiefs have the same type of sanction for their position as has the chief. They have a descent that is respected. The rule of succession is the same for sub-chiefs and headmen as it is for the chief. The eldest son of the chief wife has a preferred claim, but, if there is a son by another wife who is older, he is often chosen. Nowadays, it is becoming common for headmen to choose the most able son, to retire from office, and to present the chosen son to the chief as the successor. The chief, who must confirm the appointment, usually accepts the successor chosen by the holder of the office. Of the present sub-chiefs, six are the sons of important *vantsagila*. Whether the offices will continue to be filled on the basis of hereditary right remains to be seen. The other sanctions are also effective. They have the privilege of supplicating their ancestors for favours which affect their whole territory, particularly the privilege of praying for rain; most of them support their position by the use of all kinds of medicines, from killing medicine to medicine for increasing the number of their wives; and, while they all lack the large train of followers they used to have, the use of porters when they travel, the services of uniformed messengers, and the assistance of trained clerks make very satisfactory compensation for the old splendour.

Sub-chiefs are probably respected much as their older prototypes were. It is realized that they wield wide powers delegated by the chief; and all of them have personal claims to respect, on account of their ancestry, character, and abilities. But there is little doubt that a large amount of respect comes as a result of their official position. They exert new powers of coercion in enforcing judgements. Furthermore, their possession of tax records, court records, and clerks, and their functions as delegates of the central Government, have done more to establish their authority than have the mass of traditional sanctions.

In the performance of their official functions, there are so many individual differences that to discuss them in detail would resolve itself into gossip about their individual characters. All that can be done here is to give a general idea as to how their official duties are carried out.

THE HEHE TRIBE

As judges, the majority of them perform their tasks well. Cases are judged fairly on their merits, and, as a rule, justice is speedy and satisfactory. When this general fact is stated, many exceptions must be made. Two of the sub-chiefs are so dilatory in granting hearings that they are practically useless. A third is inclined to delay, but not to the same degree. The other six are beyond criticism in this respect.

There are other kinds of corruption. One of the sub-chiefs is apt to seek his own advantage too much. If a desirable woman is a litigant, she will have a good chance of a favourable judgement if she agrees to become one of his wives. The same sub-chief will often delay justice indefinitely until it dawns upon the plaintiff that a judicious present will hasten matters. This sort of abuse is particularly hard to detect, because the sub-chief chooses his victims carefully and will not make any such experiments upon a sophisticated or educated Hehe. Two or three others of the sub-chiefs are not completely guiltless in this respect, but the remainder are said to be always fair in their judgements.

Probably the most serious corruption arises from the fact that tribal officials always support one another. Thus, if a headman has been guilty of irregularity in his methods of tax-collection, the sub-chief will do his best to avoid hearing the case or to secure an acquittal; not because he gains any personal advantage, but because he sympathizes too much with the accused's problems and identifies himself too much with his status. This fault is understandable. The functions of a Hehe ruler are still considered indivisible, even though, in fact, they are gradually becoming less so; and it is asking much of a man to condemn as a judge the very act he would condone as an executive.

These forms of corruption can only be eradicated gradually. They are, even now, checked by three factors. The first is the fact that the sub-chief is still only the president of the court and must listen to his advisers. Their advice is often disregarded, but they cannot always be ignored. The second is the right of appeal and the fear of revision; and the third is the spread of education. As the tribal subjects become more conscious of their rights and the way to secure them, it will become more and more difficult for those possessing power to use their authority for undesirable ends.

As executives, one of the principal functions of the sub-chiefs is to assist in the collection of tax. This new function often overrides all other aspects of their duties except the judicial. The fact is unfortunate; but at the present stage of development it is difficult to see that it could be otherwise. It should be added, however, that the sub-chiefs have performed this task with remarkable honesty; and there have been few serious embezzlements of government funds. From the point of view of the subject, the sub-chiefs, as tax-collectors, are sometimes guilty of rather arbitrary measures; but these do not take extreme forms and are usually confined to putting the tax-defaulter to a succession of inconveniences. There has seldom been a suggestion of corruption; in tax-collection the corruption, as we shall see, occurs lower down in the tribal hierarchy.

Summing up the position of the sub-chiefs, their influence and their authority rest partly on their identification with the old *vantsagila*, but probably to a greater extent on their association with the newer forms of executive duties which are being developed within the tribe. Their future is thus more problematical than that of any other tribal officials. On the one hand, they may develop into a group of hereditary rulers, always in subordination to the chief, but with a recognized status. On the other, the development of the executive duties placed upon them may demand such a degree of special education, of a purely clerical nature, that men will be picked for the post regardless of descent, and they will become a branch of the tribal civil service. The latter sounds the more efficient development, but it has its own pitfalls; for the ultimate efficiency of any group of rulers depends upon the extent to which they can win the allegiance of their subjects. Without venturing to prophesy, we suggest the possibility that the Hehe are not prepared to dispense with the sanction of hereditary right.

(*d*) *The Headmen.*

The evolution of the present position of the headmen has been sketched in the last section. It now remains to indicate more precisely the nature of their authority and the extent of their functions.

In the present tribal organization, there are seventy headmen. The average number of subjects under each is therefore a little more than 1,000 (the actual numbers vary from 400 to over 2,000); and the average area of each is more than 150 square miles. In terms of the number of their subjects, they would thus seem to be rather unimportant officials. We believe this to be the exact reverse of the truth. Reasons will be advanced to indicate that they are at least as important as **any** other tribal officials, and that without them government would be a very difficult matter.

In terms of law and of administrative actuality, their tenure of office depends upon the consent of the chief and the concurrence of the District Officer. Removal is, legally, a simple matter; and many dismissals have occurred in the past few years. Positively, from the same point of view, their authority is strengthened by government recognition of their place in the tribal structure. But if this is considered the only or even the chief sanction of their office, one misreads their true significance.

In the first place they are, in the eyes of the people, more completely the representatives of the old *vantsagila* than are the present sub-chiefs. In stating this fact, it must be emphasized that native opinion is not at all precise in this respect. The sub-chiefs are also, in a sense, the inheritors of the old status; but the headmen have that status to a greater degree. Their rights, their duties, their position as intermediaries between their people and the superior authorities, all contribute to make them the direct descendants of the old *vantsagila*, the old sub-chiefs who were under the chief only. Moreover, this native view of their status is strengthened by the fact that they are, in a very real sense, the unbroken descendants of the *vantsagila*. During a generation when all central tribal authority disappeared, they were able to carry on; their territories were reduced; new-comers, formerly petty headmen, were accepted as their equals; but their authority remained unimpaired, though it operated over a smaller area and had to be shared by others. In addition, many of the headmen are the sons or grandsons of former *vantsagila*, and the authority of these families has thus been continuous.

This identification with the old *vantsagila* indirectly identifies the headmen with the old *vatwa* (the small paramount chiefs whose power was destroyed or subordinated by the Muyinga family), and their present territories with the old independent tribal territories of four generations ago. This statement is an oversimplification, of course. The Hehe know that those territories have been changed and divided; that descendants of many of the old reigning houses have become commoners; and that many new-comers have obtained authority to which their right is not hereditary. Notwithstanding these facts, there is, in Hehe belief, a remote and vague but nevertheless real identity between headmen and old *vatwa*, and between old independent tribal territories and the present areas ruled by the headmen.

This identity of old petty chief and present headman permits the operation of another sanction to their power, that of religion. Just as the chief, and the chief only, is permitted to supplicate his ancestors on matters affecting the whole tribe, so only the headman is permitted to make supplications on behalf of his community. Those headmen who are really descended from the old chiefs would seem at first sight to be the only possessors of ancestral spirits whose powers would be sufficient; for only they ruled the territories concerned. But actually, any ruling headman is considered capable of prevailing upon his ancestors in matters affecting the public good. Moreover, the general rule is that a descendant of an old chief cannot pray to his ancestors on behalf of the community, unless he is in the possession of effective political power. There are two or three men, descendants of old chiefs, to whom this rule does not apply. Although politically they are commoners, their prayers, or their ancestors' powers, are so great that they are asked annually to pray for rain. But the general rule now is that only chief, sub-chief, or headman, in actual possession of power, can offer sacrifice and prayer on behalf of the community. This sanction does not hold in some areas; Christian or Mohammedan influences are causing these beliefs to become weak; but in most areas it is still an important support to the headman's authority. Before European occupation, a sub-chief could not pray for the community without the chief's order or consent. Nowadays, he is still supposed to notify the chief when he does so; but so far as limited information indicates, this control on the part of the chief is not very effective.

The identification of the headman with the old chiefs has one very important corollary: it is the headman, not the chief, who is the owner of the land (*munya inyi*). This attribute is real, not titular. If a man wishes to change his residence or if a foreigner wishes to enter the country, it is the headman, not the chief, whose permission to settle is sought. As a general rule, this permission is not refused; the headman wishes to add to his subjects, and he is usually willing to find him a place to build his house and cultivate his plantations. But his power of refusal, if seldom exercised, is nevertheless real. If the land is not sufficient or if the applicant is notoriously a bad character, permission to settle will be refused. Permission to settle implies not only the assignment of a building plot, but the allotment of sufficient ground for cultivation. If the new-comer lives at a sufficient distance from his neighbours, the boundaries are not carefully marked. If the new-comer builds near others, his exact boundaries are indicated, and he must seek specific permission to go beyond them. This privilege of giving land to new-comers is exclusively the headman's. The chief, or the new sub-chief, may order the headman to give land to a specific person (though this is a very rare occurrence), but this overriding jurisdiction does not give them the right of assigning plots. That belongs to the headman alone, and marks him as the real possessor of the land.

The headman holds his position by hereditary right, by religious sanction, because he is the owner of the land, and also by the assent of the community. This latter fact is difficult to comprehend by European standards. The individual does not elect, in any European sense; he cannot reject by plebiscite; and he is, unless pressed, too tactful to express an overt objection. It nevertheless remains a fact that if the headman cannot rule by the assent of the community, he cannot rule effectively at all. If he is disliked actively by a large majority, a delegation will appeal for his replacement. If he is disliked passively, his commands will be disregarded. This privilege of assent works in an obscure way. Ordinarily, it is not an effective factor in selection; but it does act as a final veto on some one who is completely undesirable. and it prevents a tyrant from remaining in office. This need for the assent of the community is seldom evident to the European, partly because it is so seldom exercised. Usually a headman can secure the support of a faction, if there has been trouble; and the opposing faction, even if in the majority, will seldom make open opposition. But if the opposition is almost universal, it will make itself felt and the headman will have to go.[1]

---

[1] A few years ago a delegation waited on the District Officer and asked to have their headman removed. The then District Officer did not realize the intense forces which must have led to such a step,

In these days, the position of the headman is not sufficiently realized by his superiors. The administrative officer seldom understands it and the chief disregards it. In the olden days, this would have been impossible; the chief might be unscrupulous, but, to maintain his power, he must be alive to political realities and must keep his following by all the means at his disposal. Nowadays, the chief, backed by the Government, is apt to ignore the lessons of tribal history and to seek temporary advantage by replacing a headman and thus sacrificing tribal stability. The only remedy for this state of affairs is the evolution of constitutional checks, to replace the old caution imposed by political necessity.

Although backed by a multiplicity of sanctions, the headman does not rest content, but seeks to reinforce his power by adding to his influence in a variety of ways. He adds to his magical powers by collecting medicines as the chief used to do; and the medicines he collects add to his powers in specific ways. One headman, for example, has a medicine for killing his enemies. He is alleged to have killed, among others, ten soldiers during the War. This man became the most powerful headman in the neighbourhood, and, as a consequence, now enjoys the privileges, perquisites, and position of a sub-chief. Another headman relies chiefly on increasing the number of his wives: he has a medicine that is said to be very effective. The

and so did not grant the request. The very rarity of such an appeal made it significant.

result is that he has married twenty wives, thirteen of whom are still living with him, and he has forty surviving children. Still another has medicine for inclining people to favour his causes; he was accused several times of the embezzlement of tax money; each time (it is said) he escaped conviction by secretly administering this medicine to his judges; and if he was finally convicted and removed from office, it was due to the use of still more powerful medicines by his enemies. These examples may show the part medicine plays in building up power. Whatever may be the actual material effect of the medicine, the headman's people believe in it and respect his powers accordingly.

A headman also adds to his wealth. Opportunities for doing so are unfortunately plentiful. Old men who wish to be exempted from the tax must first present the headman with an ox before he submits their names. Presents for privileges are encouraged. The headman enjoys a considerable judicial power, but, not being head of a regularly constituted court, he is forbidden to take court fees; nevertheless these fees are still paid, though the spread of a knowledge of his status under the native authorities is causing this to die out. He still receives presents after a judgement, as a token of gratitude for a favourable decision. More specific emoluments are still paid him. When a man dies, his heirs pay the headman two shillings. This custom dates from olden days; the chief was always a sharer in the inheritance of a dead man;

when the chieftainate was destroyed, this privilege was acquired by the headmen; and it gradually came to be commuted for a regular fee of two shillings. Nowadays it is justified by the claim that it is a fee to remove the man's name from the tax list. A headman also gets a regular salary. The amount is not negligible, but it is small in relation to the perquisites of office. Most of these perquisites are abuses. Direct action can do little to stop them. They will only cease when the spread of knowledge causes the people to realize that they cannot be demanded and that their enforcement is an abuse of power.

A headman also increases his social prestige, by marrying as many wives as he can. A large number of wives adds to his comfort, on account of the amount and variety of food with which they supply him; to his social esteem, from the amount of entertainment in food and drink which he is able to offer; and to the probability of many offspring, most desirable end of all in Hehe eyes. It also adds to the number of persons related to him, and thus to the number of his adherents.

Most headmen seek their own advantage in the manner described above. Many of their privileges are illegal and tend to the development of corruption. But when one sees the multiplicity of tasks the headmen have to perform, one wonders at their moderation.

A headman exercises the same undivided powers as his ancestors did and as his superiors do: he is judge, leader, and executive of his community. As judge, his foremost function in native eyes, his position is anomalous. In actual fact, he hears a vast number of cases, although legally[1] he is not a judge at all and has no power to enforce his decisions. In addition to hearing and deciding cases himself, he frequently holds a preliminary inquiry into cases he must afterwards send on to his superiors. To understand how this anomalous system works, one must understand the function of the leader as judge in Hehe society.

Primarily, a Hehe leader is more arbitrator than judge. True, his efficiency is to a great extent estimated by his legal ability, but the ability required is that of leading public opinion. Thus a headman sitting in court is not a magistrate whose word is all-powerful within his warrant, but the chairman of a court, who must listen to the facts, listen to the opinions of his advisers and assistants, and eventually announce, not his personal judgement, but the judgement of the assembly. It is probable that this is the fundamental aspect of all Hehe judicial meetings; they are organized expressions of public opinion when any dispute arises. With the growth of a complex system of authority, superior officials are apt to be arbitrary in their methods if not in their judgements, while the lower courts retain the more purely communal principles of judicial procedure. At any rate, a litigant in a headman's court, even though he knows he cannot be forced to accept the headman's judgement, gene-

[1] The only legally established courts are those of the chief and the sub-chiefs. See above, p. 11.

rally does accept it, because it is an expression of public opinion.

Those constituting the headman's court are usually representative of the leading men in the community. There are, first, the *vakalani*, the subordinates and delegates of the headman, whose other functions are to be discussed shortly. There are, in addition, a number of men who have no official or pseudo-official position in the community, but whose legal skill is a matter of public recognition. To serve in the headman's court is a reward in itself. All Hehe of ability pride themselves on their skill in law. A man's intelligence is judged by his forensic ability. Thus, in a community of lawyers, to serve in the headman's court is at once a duty, a privilege, and a recognition of superiority.

In such a court, just decisions are generally given. Causes are argued skilfully, discussed at length, and judged on their merits. The cases dealt with show some variety. Marital and family disputes, petty theft, adultery, slander and abuse,[1] fighting, and suits for debts are some of the common ones. These are not different from the disputes heard in the regularly constituted sub-chief's court; they differ only in the magnitude of the offence and in the nature of the judgement. It is only the petty cases which are heard in the headman's court; the more serious ones are sent on to the sub-chief. And the only judgement can be an order to pay compensation; it is only the legally

[1] See below, p. 125.

established courts which can inflict penalties of fine or imprisonment.

The legal position of the headmen's courts has only been understood by the Hehe in the last three or four years. Before 1926, the headmen were accustomed to trying all cases except those connected with serious crime. The advantage of going to the regularly constituted sub-chiefs' courts is now better understood, and the headmen themselves send up more cases than formerly. The practice is not uniform; some headmen still try serious cases; there is evidence that some of them still grant divorces, for example. But, on the whole, the headmen have learned to recognize their limitations and are beginning to show some discrimination in selecting cases with which they may deal themselves and in sending on the more important ones.

The headman's court also performs a useful psychological function. It enables grievances to be aired in a manner which would not be possible in a regularly constituted court. When a litigant brings a case before a headman, it often implies his desire to be vindicated by public opinion rather than a wish to seek material compensation. For example, a woman was seen by her husband to be talking to a man outside their house, in the dark. Without making inquiries, the husband administered a beating. It turned out that the man was the woman's brother. She accused her husband before the headman of beating her 'without cause'. The husband publicly admitted his fault. The woman then announced that she did not want compensation; she only wished her character to be cleared publicly. The hearing of a great many cases such as this keeps the peace in the community.

The judicial activities of the headman are thus essential to social life. They enable disputes to be settled in a traditional manner and provide a socially recognized means of stating grievances. They are indispensable, too, on account of the number of cases they deal with. If there were no headmen's courts, the legally constituted courts of the sub-chiefs could not deal with all the litigation in the tribe. The headmen's courts leave only the more serious cases for the sub-chiefs, thus allowing the latter more time to deal with them.

The greatest weakness of the headmen's courts is that they have no power to enforce their decisions. A litigant may agree to pay the compensation ordered and then simply do nothing. Two factors minimize this disadvantage. First, most people do pay, if only to settle the matter without further trouble. Secondly, the successful suitor, if he obtains no satisfaction, can always go to the sub-chief's court and have the case retried. If he is forced to such a course, the fact that a favourable judgement has been passed by the headman will stand him in good stead in the eyes of the sub-chief, even though it will not be the main consideration. Incidentally, this right to go to the higher court very considerably decreases the possibility of corruption on the part of the headman.

Although the native regards the leader primarily as

a judge, yet he has many duties as an executive, one of which bids fair, in these days, to overshadow his judicial duties. This particular function is the part he plays in the collection of the hut and poll tax. By law,[1] his share in this task should be a small one. Every tax-payer is supposed to take his tax to the office of the sub-chief, get his receipt, and so perform his public duty with a minimum of trouble to all concerned. In reality, this ideal is seldom attained. The headman, if the tax money is available, often collects it himself (although he has no authority to do so) and sends it to his sub-chief; he fears that otherwise it would be spent. In addition to this, he devotes a considerable amount of time each year to persuading his people to go to work or to sell their produce or stock, in order to obtain their tax money. The result is that the collection of hut and poll tax is regarded as of undue importance both by the headman and by his people.

Many other executive duties fall his way: the carrying out of the chief's orders; the collection of porters for officials on tour; and the preservation of the peace. In general, the headman is indispensable to government; he carries out the orders of those above him; and he is regarded by his people as the medium through whom all orders come and through whom the community can give expression to its needs.

So far, the headman has been considered as a useful

[1] Collectors of hut and poll tax are required to be specially appointed, *vide* section 2 of the Hut and Poll Tax Ordinance, op. cit., p. 10. Headmen are not collectors under the Ordinance.

instrument of government. To understand further his significance in the political organization, it is necessary to give a more careful description of the community he rules. The headman's community is made up of a number of local units, each of which is called a *lilungulu*. This term we shall translate by the term 'settlement'. A settlement is not a village, but is composed of a number of houses scattered irregularly over an area of country which may vary in size from two to ten square miles. Some settlements have only one house, others two or three, but an ordinary settlement contains from ten to twenty houses. Certain factors cause a concentration. Thus, where the ground is exceptionally fertile, the houses will be close together. Often, too, a number of households grow up around a headman. Where this occurs, the settlement approximates to a village. But the large majority of the Hehe live in the manner indicated. These settlements are distinct units in that they have recognized boundaries and names; and the members have a belief that they form a community distinct from other communities. Where most of the members of the settlement are bound together by kinship ties, the feeling of unity is intensified. But the settlement has no common head and no common activities. It is thus a very weak social unit and is not in any sense a unit of government. The smallest unit of local government is a number of such settlements under a subordinate of the headman called an *mkalani*.[1] Though the

[1] From the Swahili *karani*, a clerk, and thus an official with

mkalani has thus a claim to be called the head of the smallest unit of government, yet when one understands the relation existing between him and his people on the one hand, and between him and his superior, the headman, on the other, it becomes apparent that his community is only in a very limited sense a community or a unit of government, and that the smallest effective political unit is the larger community administered by the headman.

When considering the complicated system of subdividing a community which generally consists of no more than 1,000 to 1,500 people, it should be borne in mind that these people are scattered over a large area of country,[1] and that the complex duties of the headman require a considerable amount of assistance. A headman must therefore have a large staff of assistants, the *vakalani*, who are of at least three kinds. There are the greater *vakalani* among whom the country is divided. A headman has from four to eight of these, each with his area assigned to him. The areas so assigned have no particular sociological or historical significance; the borders are drawn merely as a matter of convenience and may easily be changed. These greater *vakalani* have, in turn, their own subordinates; and if a subordinate has a large enough area, he may also have his subordinate.

subordinate powers. The term *mkalani* replaces the old Hehe term *mpakasi*, which fell into disuse because of its resemblance to the Swahili *mpagazi*, a porter.

[1] The density of population in the whole tribe is only seven per square mile.

In addition to the territorial and subordinate *vakalani*, there are a number of *vakalani* who have no area under their control, but who act as delegates and messengers of the headman. In the olden days, they would have been called *vanya mulyango*, 'those who belong to the doorway'. Nowadays, their authority is considerable, and one of them is the immediate subordinate of the headman, representing him when he is absent and assisting him when present. Their general duties are to convey orders to the outlying parts, to see that the orders are carried out, to help in the collection of the tax, and to assist in the settlement of disputes when the headman holds court. They and the territorial *vakalani*, in short, are a group of delegates and subordinates to aid the headman in the execution of all his duties.

It is when the *vakalani* form members of a local court that the nature of their influence is seen most clearly. It has been noted that a headman is the chairman of a court and that he must lead public opinion. The *vakalani* are the chief representatives of public opinion, and they play an important part in conducting the case—cross-questioning the witnesses, advocating one side or the other, and formulating the decisions. A headman will seldom oppose their united opinion. For instance, a woman suing for divorce gave the headman two shillings to 'help' her; the *vakalani* were unanimous that she had inadequate grounds, and the divorce was refused. (The headman did not, however, return the bribe.) The amount of influence they exert varies, of course, with individual differences of character. An extremely powerful and dominating headman is able to impose his will on the group; an exceptionally able *mkalani* can exert more influence than all his fellows. But, in general, a judicial decision is an honest expression of the group judgement and ultimately of public opinion.

The *vakalani* not only assist the judicial decisions of the headman, but hold courts of their own; this applies particularly to the territorial *vakalani*. Petty cases are often brought to them first. The number of cases heard will depend upon the reputation of the individual *mkalani* for his legal skill; and a few may hear as many cases as a headman. But as a rule people prefer to go to the headman. The petty judicial work of the *vakalani* is often very similar to police work; they prevent or stop fights and give assistance in case of trouble. Thus a man accused his wife of entertaining a lover in his absence and began to beat her. She ran away and appealed to the nearest *mkalani*. He came back with her and was immediately accused of being the lover in question. He and the woman went away and returned with another *mkalani*. The husband was admonished and ordered to stop beating his wife. As soon as the two *vakalani* had left, the husband began beating the wife again for daring to tell them, whereupon she again ran away and appealed to them. Thoroughly annoyed, the *vakalani* gave the husband a beating, and warned him that if he struck his wife again the consequences would be still more drastic. Such violent exercise of authority is, however, seldom necessary; in most cases an admonition has the required effect.

The *vakalani* are thus indispensable to local government. But two limitations minimize their power. First, they are unpaid. This would not necessarily matter, but in a tribe where most functionaries get some sort of financial recognition, and where a certain minimum income is necessary to pay the tax and to buy clothes, it is an important consideration. It may be a matter of surprise that men on whom such a burden of work falls should carry on for no material reward; but the advantages, though immaterial, are real enough. The *vakalani* occupy a position of authority, one which is respected by the whole community; their judicial functions are a public recognition of their legal abilities, a recognition desired by all ambitious Hehe; and they are exempted from unpleasant tasks, such as turning out for communal labour and carrying loads for government or tribal officials. These inducements are sufficient to attract able men, for the present at any rate; whether they will be sufficient in the future will be a matter for serious consideration.

The second limitation is that they occupy their positions entirely at the will of the headman, and the individual *mkalani* has no official recognition by the tribal authorities. They are, in fact, only individually appointed delegates of an individual headman; and, if a new headman is installed, he will, in some cases, replace all existing *vakalani* by appointees of his own. This does not mean that any one is suitable for the office; they must be chosen with some care, for upon them depends the headman's ability to administer his community efficiently; but in the last resort the appointment depends entirely upon the headman.

The *vakalani* are chosen on a basis of kinship to the headman, for individual ability, or because of their family importance. On the basis of kinship, a headman usually chooses one or two of his brothers to live near him, to act as his immediate delegates and to be his authorized messengers. If one of them is of sufficient ability, he will generally be chosen to act as principal deputy. In Wasa, when old Makologoto retired, he had his eldest son installed as headman in his place, and he chose two other sons to reside near the eldest to assist him. The post of principal deputy alternates between the two younger brothers. One of them is able, but independent of his brother's influence; the other is rather stupid, but subservient; and the headman gives now one, now the other, the principal place, in accordance with the outcome of the latest quarrel or the latest stupidity. The headman of Tanangozi has chosen one brother as his principal deputy.

At other times, ability governs the choice. The headman of Malangali has as his principal deputy a man not related to him at all, but whose abilities command respect and ensure the efficient carrying out of instructions. Usually, ability counts more than kinship when it comes to choosing the territorial *vakalani*. These are frequently men in the prime of life, who command the respect of their people.

It is also important to the headman to gain the support and the co-operation of the more important families of the community. Families may be important on account of ancient eminence, present wealth, or a general high level of ability. The important fact is that the family as a whole has the respect of the community. A wise headman always tries to gain their support by associating them with himself in the task of government. The most striking example we studied intimately was that of the VaKihwele family of Wasa. It is large, and in the olden days one of its members had been an important deputy of Mpangile, a brother of chief Mkwawa, who ruled that area. Another member of the family was one of the most noted elephant-hunters in the tribe. The eldest male, the present head of the family, had retired some years ago; that is, he had withdrawn from direct participation in public affairs. Before his retirement, he had been *mkalani* of a large section of the headman's community (140 out of 300 tax-payers). This position was passed on to the eldest male of the next generation, the son of the old man's brother. A younger male, son of the old man himself, lived near the headman, acting at once as delegate to the headman and to his own family. In 1931 the family became embroiled with the headman and resigned as a group.

The *vakalani* are thus far from negligible. They can

make or unmake the effective authority of the headman; they are indispensable as instruments of government; but they are, after all, only delegates of the headman. They owe their appointments directly to him and can be removed when he wills. Hence their areas of authority are barely units of government; and the smallest unit of effective and organized government is the whole community ruled by the headman.

This indicates the final and possibly the greatest significance of the headman in the political life of the tribe. It is the local organization which is prior to, and a necessary basis of, the larger organization of the tribe. Community bonds are not the strongest social bonds among the Hehe; kinship bonds always take precedence. These bonds are simply the sum of all the obligations assumed by all members of the tribe towards others related to them by blood or affinity, and they are accepted as being natural, inevitable, and indestructible. The bonds holding together members of the community are different, if not in kind, at least in degree. The obligations towards one who is merely a fellow member of the community are less complex and less enduring than those one owes to a kinsman. In a limited but real sense a non-kinsman is always a potential enemy, or at least a member of a potentially hostile group. Consequently, for a communal life, new sanctions are developed, and the organization of the headman's community forms a necessary prerequisite to the organization of the tribe.

(e) *The Subject.*

So much for the tribal authorities. It remains to indicate the position of the subject with relation to these authorities.

For the greater part of his time, the subject may pursue his social and economic interests; and in the pursuit of these interests, he may expect the protection of the tribal authorities against interference with his person, his activities, his property, and his reputation. As will be discussed more fully in the account of native law, if any of these privileges are violated he can claim compensation; and the right to make the claim goes far to preserve their observance.

The subject is also permitted freedom of movement within the tribe (and, as a matter of fact, within all the Tanganyika Territory). He may travel where he will without let or hindrance. This is a privilege much appreciated by the Hehe; few of them leave their tribal boundaries, but within them they travel frequently and widely. They may also change their residence as they please. There is only one limitation to this privilege. A Hehe may decide to leave the place where he is living; but to build a new house, he must obtain the consent of the headman of the new area; in other words he cannot be forbidden to leave a place, but he must get permission to enter a new community as a resident. This limitation actually implies nothing but a formality, as a headman is always willing to receive a new subject unless he is notoriously a bad neighbour. And, as mentioned, permission to settle includes the right to build a house, and to a grant of land sufficient for all ordinary needs. So that, in fact, within his tribe, a Hehe has no political or economic restrictions upon his right to change residence.

The negative obligations upon the Hehe are the ordinary social obligations to refrain from breaking the law and to abstain from infringing the rights of others.

Probably those things which loom largest to the Hehe in his relation to the Government are the positive obligations which he must fulfil. First of these, in his mind, is his obligation to pay the tax. His ability to pay this tax and the change which it implies in his life will be dealt with in connexion with economics. It is sufficient to say here that, while it is definitely a big effort, it is well within the means of the average tribesman.

If the only positive obligation to the tribal authorities and the Government were the payment of tax, the Hehe would have limited cause for grumbling. They have other petty, but indefinitely recurring, obligations. First, there are tribal public works. These are simple and are chiefly confined to making rough roads and paths. Even this would be negligible if they were paid for these tasks. In theory they are paid. A headman is given money or salt, ordered to supervise a certain task, and is supposed to divide what he gets among his helpers. Actually, the latter seldom see any of it. But the obligation disliked most of all is the liability to carry loads. If voluntary labour is not available, porters must be found to carry the loads of government officers touring on duty and of tribal officials. Porters for government officers are always paid; those carrying the loads of tribal officials, seldom. But, in native eyes, most unpleasant aspect of all is the incidence of the duty. Headmen are too apt to choose those they do not like to perform this undesirable task. It is bad enough if they are paid, a little worse if they are not.[1] And an equally unpleasant aspect of this obligation is the unexpectedness with which the blow falls; any one is apt to be told one day that he must carry loads the next.

Other lesser obligations exist. The privileges of the chief to have his house built and his plantations cultivated imply corresponding obligations on his subjects to perform these tasks. And there are emergency obligations. The Hehe must be prepared to turn out to fight fires, to combat locusts, and to assemble for public purposes on the order of the chief. With these duties no one need quarrel. There are, however, certain illegal obligations which annoy. Practically any European travelling through the country on foot can demand and get porters. There is no law to back this demand and no legal remedy for the European if

---

[1] In 1933 this obligation became much less unpopular in native eyes. Work was so scarce that volunteers for porterage were plentiful. The above remarks apply more to the years 1929, 1930, and 1931.

he does not get his porters, but a headman seldom refuses him. In brief, there are a multitude of minor obligations, some legal, some illegal, which are demanded of the subject. But apart from the obligation to pay tax, the Hehe are little disturbed by their public duties, and an average three or four days' work a year would amply fulfil them.

We have tried to describe the political organization of the tribe, showing its weaknesses as well as its strength, its abuses as well as its essential functions. In case the weaknesses and the abuses have been overemphasized, it must be said that the structure functions, on the whole, with a considerable degree of efficiency. There is some petty corruption, but there are no serious abuses. There are some miscarriages of justice, but, in the vast majority of cases, judgements are impartial. There are some roughnesses in the executive sphere, but the Hehe have had only one generation in which to learn many lessons of living in peace; and these roughnesses will decrease as the tribesmen learn to fulfil their obligations and at the same time to assert their individual rights.

2. KINSHIP ORGANIZATION

This account of kinship is by no means a full one and does not attempt to comply with the standards of modern anthropology. The reason for this lies in the limitations imposed by the terms of the experiment; that is, the extent to which each of the various fields of native culture is dealt with is determined by the questions of the administrator. It is the considered opinion of the administrator that an extensive knowledge of kinship is not necessary for the particular problems facing him, and that all he requires is a knowledge sufficient to understand certain other fields of culture. The anthropologist believes that a more extensive account than that here presented would prove itself useful; but, by the terms agreed upon, there is no justification for a comprehensive analysis. The account here given, therefore, is only a brief outline, with such occasional expansion as is indicated by certain specific questions.

(*a*) *The Family.*

Among the Hehe, the fundamental kinship bonds are those formed within the elementary family, consisting of father, mother, and children. The strongest social ties are those uniting parent and child, and children of the same parents. But among the Hehe there are many children with only one common parent. First, in a polygynous society, there are many children who have a common father but different mothers. Secondly, divorce is frequent, and there are many cases of children with a common mother but different fathers. The elementary kinship terms are not restricted to these groups, but are extended to a larger circle of kindred. To understand Hehe kinship, therefore, it is necessary to understand, first, the nature and strength of the bonds uniting the elementary family; and secondly, the degree to which similar bonds are effective in the larger group.

In the elementary family the father is the person in authority. He makes, or at least assents to, the important decisions affecting his children's lives. He supervises the education of his sons, deciding when they must begin tending cattle (the first serious task of boyhood), when they must begin to cultivate the soil, and when they must learn other tasks, such as building houses. His control over his daughters is less, but his consent must be given before they can marry. He states the amount of *mafungu* (bride-wealth) to be handed over, and he receives it from his daughters' husbands at the time of marriage. After his daughters are married, he continues to be protector and head of the family, and they always appeal to him in marital or material difficulties. This system of responsibilities involves property obligations: he must help his son to pay the *mafungu* when he marries, and he must refund his daughter's *mafungu* if she is divorced.

Certain social attributes are derived from the father. From him, his children get their *mulongo* (clan-name), *mulugutitso* or *mwidikitso* (praise-name), and *mtsilo* (avoidance). The *mulongo* indicates membership in a large patrilineal group and is sometimes used as a term of address; thus a male member of the Muyinga clan is Mwa-Muyinga, a female is Se-Muyinga. The praise-name is a polite form of address. The avoidance is usually that of eating a certain animal or certain parts of animals, but it may be avoidance of a vegetable food or of food cooked by a certain kind of firewood. These patrilineally derived attributes belong to the person, man or woman, for life. Marriage does not alter them in the slightest degree. Membership in the social group to which the father belongs is accepted as inevitable and natural; and when the father dies, the bulk of his valuable property (cattle or money) is divided between his children, the sons getting a larger share, but all getting something.

The father thus owes his children a complex of services, protection and material help and aid in emergencies. In return he is owed obedience. The obedience is not absolute, but is regulated by custom. A father cannot give an order which does not conform to the Hehe concept of what is fitting; nor would a child be expected to obey such an order. For example, a father can refuse a suitor for his daughter's hand, but he cannot force an unwanted suitor upon her.

The relationship between mother and child is somewhat different. The mother has the duty of looking after the children when they are young, and in return has the right of keeping her small children with her in case of a separation. Even later, when a child is old enough to be claimed by the husband, she has the right to have it visit her, and her brother can enforce this claim for her. Materially, she has the right to a third part of her daughter's *mafungu*; and she has the corresponding obligation to contribute a third of her son's *mafungu*. This is frequently done for her by her brother. Her children inherit from her, but this is not as important as paternal inheritance, as women have relatively little property. She conveys no formal social attributes to her children, but relationship to the more immediate circle of the mother's family implies a system of intimate obligations. She has certain authority; her consent must always be gained before a daughter can be married; but generally her authority is much less than that of the father. On the other hand, her influence is often greater; and it is no uncommon phenomenon to see a grown son supporting his mother against his father in cases of dispute. The children of one father and one mother form a strongly united group. As between brothers, there is a close community interest in the furtherance of family ends and the promotion of family eminence; and brothers frequently build their homes close together and so form small concentrations in the scattered Hehe settlements. Sisters also feel closely united throughout their lives. They depend upon the same person for protection; and, where circumstances permit, they assist each other in the rearing of their children.

As between brothers and sisters, there is a double relation. On the one hand, there are the intimate bonds which developed during childhood. These find specific expression in the continuation of their interdependence after marriage. The brother is the natural and legal guardian of his sister after marriage, if the father is aged or dead. He protects her in trouble; he refunds the *mafungu* in case of divorce; and his assistance is always at hand in an emergency. The strongest and most enduring bond between a man and a woman of the same generation is that between brother and sister, surpassing that between husband and wife. The latter relationship, though intimate, may be broken; that between brother and sister is indissoluble.

On the other hand, the strong incest barrier makes certain intimacies impossible. Children are taught when very young that certain words or acts, which are permitted ordinarily, are not permitted between brother and sister. As they grow older, these barriers increase and their significance is realized. A boy must not utter sexual words in his sister's presence and he must not touch her clothing; a girl must run away if her brother is doing or saying anything which suggests sex. This barrier does not extend to pretending ignorance of the sex activities of the other. Each can be cognizant of the marital or extramarital affairs of the other; but, within the limits which custom decrees, the incest bar is rigid.

Thus brother and sister are bound together by a mass of common interests, privileges, and obligations and are kept apart in all that pertains to the incest bar. This is reflected in the precise significances attached to the term of relationship, *muhatsa*. It is the reciprocal term of reference and address: a brother calls his sister *muhatsa*, a sister calls her brother *muhatsa*. In speech, *muhatsa* means one with whom one is intimate, whom one protects, and to whom one is bound by many ties; and it is applied by men to all kindred women of their generation, when that particular aspect of the relationship is stressed. When it is contrasted with the term *muhitsi*, it implies a kinswoman whom one may not marry; *muhitsi* is a kinswoman whom one may marry.[1] If one does not marry a particular *muhitsi*, however, one may refer to her and address her as *muhatsa*, unless called upon to define the relationship more exactly.

In polygynous households, the general principle is that one owes to a half-brother or half-sister the same obligations that exist in the case of a full brother or sister, but to a less degree. As children of the same father, all have the same clan-name, with associated attributes, and the same interests in their family eminence. But as children of different mothers, the intimacies of early childhood and common association with the same group of maternal kindred are lacking. To take but one way in which this limitation of obligation finds expression: a brother must protect and provide for his sister if she is in difficulties. This compulsion is both moral and legal in the case of a full brother. In the case of a half-brother there is less moral and no legal compulsion, unless the woman has no full brother, in which case the half-brother is legally liable. A man is considered a good brother if he helps his half-sister, but there is no socially irresistible compulsion to do so.

[1] There has been no attempt here to give the nomenclature of kinship, since it is meaningless to the reader without a complete account of all each word implies. Only the two words *muhatsa* and *muhitsi* will be analysed, as examples of the way in which Hehe kinship works.

In the case of a woman who has had two or more successive husbands and therefore two or more groups of children, one can assess the relative strength of the maternal and paternal bond. Each group of children belongs to a different paternal clan; each has a different social position, following that of the various fathers; yet it is found that the bond uniting children of one mother is stronger than that uniting those of one father. This is a socially accepted fact and has significant effects in everyday life. Thus, excluding those both of whose parents are common, one finds more sons of one mother living together than sons of one father. This is but one example of many. It may then be stated that, as regards immediate and intimate kinship bonds, relationship with the mother is more significant than relationship with the father; although, considering the family as a whole, clan-membership and material community of interests strengthen relationship with the father.

The nature of the kinship bonds in the elementary family gives form to the relationship with a larger group of kindred. Thus, on the mother's side, the child enters into relationship with his mother's sisters. Since the services they perform for him are similar in kind to those performed by his mother, he also calls them mothers. But the mother's brother is in a different position. Not being a woman, he does not function in any degree as a mother to his sister's children. Not belonging to the father's family, he cannot exert regular authority. He is, however, a person in authority in the mother's family, and therefore a special kind of relationship arises. He can intervene to protect or to aid the child in certain circumstances, when it is the mother's duty to do so but when she is socially debarred because she is a woman. Thus a child ill-treated at home will frequently take refuge with his maternal uncle. Among the Hehe, this particular relationship does not allow familiarity; the maternal uncle is treated with a ceremonial respect because he is a man and in a position of authority, even though that authority cannot be exerted directly. This relationship between an individual and his maternal uncle remains the same throughout their common lives.

On the father's side, the father's brothers are called fathers, because they are direct possessors of the family authority; and if the real father dies, one of them will be the child's legal guardian. The father's sister, like the mother's brother, is the object of a particular relationship. She belongs to the authority-possessing family, but, being a woman, she cannot exert authority herself. She is thus treated with a ceremonial respect. Her functions towards her brother's children are vague and are confined to general interest in their welfare, resulting in assistance in emergencies.

The relationship between a child and his grandparents is easy and lacks ceremony. During early childhood, his maternal grandmother, less often his paternal grandmother, is very closely associated with his upbringing. She often takes entire care of him for months, even for years, at a time. Although a grandfather has no direct authority over his grandchildren, his influence may be considerable. A young girl may refuse suitors of whom her grandparents do not approve; or she may defy her parents and run off with a man whom she knows her grandparents like. Also, a paternal grandfather who has attained a position of great respect in the community may strongly influence the decision of a grandson in many matters.

As has been mentioned above, the child calls a number of people in his parents' generation 'fathers' and 'mothers', the most important groups so designated being his father's brothers and his mother's sisters. The children of these people he calls 'brothers' and 'sisters'. Although these terms, derived from the elementary family, are extended, the relationship to these more distant brothers and sisters is not identical with that existing between him and the other children of his own father or mother. While not identical, however, the ties are similar. He has an obligation to help these more distant brothers in time of trouble and to enter into economic relationship with them. As for the sisters, there exists a strict prohibition, seldom disregarded, which prevents him from marrying or having intercourse with any woman he calls *muhatsa* (sister), however distant the kinship.

As was also mentioned above, the child does not refer to his mother's brother and his father's sister as 'father' or 'mother'. There exist separate terms of address for them. Consequently, their children are not called 'brothers' and 'sisters', but each of them, male or female, is called *muhitsi*. His relationships with them do not differ markedly from those with his classificatory brothers and sisters, with the one important exception that he may marry a female *muhitsi*, a common form of marriage among the Hehe.

Two facts emerge from these few examples of Hehe kinship usage. The first is that kinship terms belonging primarily to the elementary family are extended to a wider group of kindred; and the second that these terms are not extended to all close kindred, but that there are different kinds of kinship, according to the nature as well as to the degree of relationship.

The terms designating the elementary family extend very far; people who have a common great grandfather, in direct male or female descent, may still call each other 'brother' and 'sister'. The general principle is that some identity of function is expressed, although it may be extremely attenuated. Thus the term 'father', applied to a distant kinsman, may convey nothing more than a recognition of the kinship bond, together with a formal respect.

With regard to the nature, as distinct from the degree, of relationship, it is not necessary to discuss further the difference between a father's brother and a mother's brother, and between a father's sister and a mother's sister. It is sufficient that the differences between these groups and between their children have been indicated, so that the general principles determining these relationships may be discussed. The primary determinant of the nature of kinship is whether it depends upon the father's line or the mother's line; a second is whether the relationship involves people of opposite sex; and a third is the emphasis placed on patrilineal descent.

A child receives his or her clan-name (*mulongo*) from the father, along with the associated social attributes; and it is from the father that social status and wealth are inherited. This is not to deny the closeness of the bond with the mother's family. It is fully as intimate as that with the father's family. But relationship with kindred on the maternal side becomes less effective as the degree of kinship becomes more distant; and it eventually ceases to have any effect and is forgotten when the relationship is distant. Direct relationship, depending upon patrilineal descent, cannot, however, be similarly forgotten. Since descent is counted patrilineally and is, so to speak, labelled by possession of the *mulongo* and what goes with it, kinship through the father is effective in regard to very remote kindred. And, in addition, all people counting direct patrilineal descent from some common male ancestor constitute an easily identifiable group. This group may be called a clan.

The clan, then, is a group of people bound together by belief in direct paternal descent from a common ancestor. They have in common, also, their *mulongo* or clan-name, a praise-name, and an avoidance. They have mutual obligations. The principal of these is negative: clan members cannot intermarry.

If the exact degree of kinship is known, a man addresses a woman of his clan by the appropriate title 'aunt', 'sister', or 'daughter'; if the exact relationship is not known, he addresses her as 'daughter'. Thus the incest bar is generally observed; no violations of it have come to our notice. The other obligations are vague and may be summed up as consisting of support in trouble, hospitality, and a recognition of kinship. They are not compulsive, and usually resolve themselves into the fact that a visiting fellow clansman is more apt to receive generous hospitality than one who is not a clansman.

A clan is neither a local nor a functional unit. Members of a clan are scattered all over the tribe, and there is no clan home. Members of a clan do not assemble for ceremonial, economic, or social purposes. Hence a clan is not a unit of great social significance. It is a limited factor for social unity; the fact that a fellow clansman may possibly be found in distant parts of the tribal area makes these parts seem less foreign than they might otherwise appear; but this function is performed passively, and there is never any special emphasis laid on it. Moreover, a clan is not large enough to be represented in all areas. It is probable that there are no more than 300 or 400 members in a clan; and in a tribe numbering over 86,000 it is impossible for any clan to be represented in all communities.

Clans are in constant process of subdivision. A man in a group of brothers may at some period decide to count their descent from their father. In a generation or two there thus grows up a paternal lineage, which differs from a clan in that the degree of relationship of one member to another is known exactly. In several more generations the lineage will expand into a clan and new divisions will occur. The *mulongo* is thus changed, but the praise-name and the avoidance remain the same as those of the original clan; and it will be several generations before the relationship to the latter clan is forgotten or ignored.

The clan thus grows from the emphasis placed upon paternal descent and from the feeling of social identity which develops. It is a factor for social integration, but is of no political importance.

Hehe kinship obligations are both specific and general. There are specific obligations to very close kindred. We have tried to indicate their nature in discussing such relationships as those existing between father and children, or between child and maternal uncle. The general obligations are owed to these closer kindred and also to kindred more distantly related. These general obligations, briefly, are to assist a kinsman as against a non-kinsman; to give aid in trouble; to extend hospitality; and to give specified assistance in economic enterprises. This latter duty is not unlimited. Under ordinary conditions, a man must help a kinsman to plant his crops, to build his house, and to perform certain other heavy tasks. The amount of assistance given is limited in three ways. It cannot be more than a day at a time; it is not required if the kinsman lives at a distance; and native beer (*ugimbi*) must be supplied in return for the labour provided. It is a frequently recurring, but not necessarily an onerous, obligation.

Though kinship is the strongest social bond among the Hehe, it is not the only one. Members of a community owe certain obligations to each other. These obligations sometimes conflict with the obligations owed to kindred. For example, a man must visit a close kinsman if he is ill, if there has been a death in the family, or if there is an important family matter to be decided; and such demands must sometimes be complied with at the expense of community obligations. On the other hand, the bonds of kinship may be used to reinforce the community bonds. In any small settlement or group of settlements, there are usually a few families who are strong numerically or in social importance. For example, at Isele, the Mbwelwa family have been settled longer and have increased in numbers more than any other. The sons have built their homesteads there and the daughters have married members of other families in the area; and newer families tend to emphasize their relationship to them, whether by blood or by marriage. They assume the economic obligations, the social duties, and the legal responsibilities associated with kinship. This does not mean that obligations to close kindred living at a distance are neglected; the Hehe are very meticulous in the discharge of their kinship obligations. But it does mean that the fact of nearness and of membership in the same community emphasizes the bonds of kinship existing within that community. They are reinforced by the contact of everyday life, whereas kinsmen at a distance are ignored until some specific event brings the relationship again to notice. At the same time, kinship reinforces the community bond, and, in a community where there exist many kinship bonds, each bond strengthens the others.

The brevity of this sketch does not allow space to indicate how this mass of obligations works out in practice. The variations are innumerable; the interplay of individual character and the variety of circumstances make any generalization subject to hundreds of exceptions. We have only tried to outline the general principles of kinship and to point out that it is still probably the strongest social bond among the Hehe. Although kinship obligations are owed in their entirety only to those closely related, yet it is believed that these obligations are owed in some degree to all known kindred, however remote; and, while specific obligations are few, yet it is believed that the bond should never be ignored.

(*b*) *Marriage.*

The relationship between husband and wife is the basis of the elementary family and is therefore indispensable to the whole organization of kinship. At the same time it stands apart from kinship. The latter implies the existence of bonds which are natural and which nothing can dissolve; the marriage bond is more intimate than any other while it lasts, but it can be dissolved. Hehe marriage involves for both parties the acceptance of a complex of obligations, greater than the obligations owed elsewhere; but, at the same time, each of the partners retains undiminished membership in his or her own family and can always appeal to it when in trouble.

When a man wishes to marry a woman, he must first gain her consent. When assured of this, he sends an intermediary to her parents, first to the mother, then to the father. A ceremonial delay ensues; but if the parents consent, a day is finally named for the betrothal. At the betrothal, the woman is asked by her parents to accept the betrothal hoe; her public acceptance of this signifies her formal consent and that of her parents. The second part of the ceremony is given over to the settlement of outstanding disputes between the two families. Since marriage is assumed to involve the creation of a union between two potentially hostile groups, all quarrels must be ended by the payment of suitable compensation. In the settlement of these disputes, the family of the woman is the judicial council. It is an axiom of Hehe marriage that the man is the suppliant; it is a favour to him that the parents consent to give him their daughter; and if he does not want her, there are many other possible husbands. Under these circumstances, the family of the woman is in a position of superiority, and they therefore compose existing quarrels on their own terms.

The third part of the ceremony is devoted to a settlement of the *mafungu*, the bride-wealth, which must be handed over to the parents by the bridegroom. The amount is stated by the father, is discussed by other members of the bride's family, is confirmed in its final form by the father, and is always agreed upon by the groom's intermediaries. Numerous considerations vary the amount, but a normal *mafungu* is 2 cows, 1 bull, 2 sheep, 2 or 3 hoes, and a sum of money ranging from 12 to 20 shillings. When this is settled, the formal part of the betrothal ceremony is over. From this time on the man refers to the woman as *munu vangu*, 'my wife'. She does not go to live with him, but he has a definite legal status in regard to her. If the marriage does not take place, he can claim damages; and if she commits adultery, he may exact compensation both from her and from the adulterer.

The *mafungu*, which is normally handed over on the day of the wedding, serves to stabilize the marriage. It tends to ensure that the husband complies with his obligations to his wife and that the wife remains with the husband. In case of divorce, it must be returned. Since the money value of the property so handed over is equivalent to the amount a man ordinarily earns in two or three years, it is a considerable transaction; and marriage is a matter which cannot be lightly undertaken.[1]

---

[1] Cf. G. Gordon Brown, 'Bride-wealth among the Hehe', *Africa*, vol. v, no. 2, pp. 145–57, where the function of *mafungu* is discussed more fully.

Within the last few years, the chief has attempted to limit the amount of *mafungu* to one head of cattle, a small money payment, and two hoes. In the olden days, commoners could only demand two hoes as *mafungu*, so that it is in accordance with Hehe custom for the chief to exert his authority to limit the amount, but it is not a simple matter to estimate the probable consequences of enforcing such a rule to-day. It is certain that there would be an initial opposition to strict enforcement on the part of the fathers of marriageable daughters, whose family prestige is asserted by the privilege of demanding a high payment. This opposition would continue, in spite of attempted control through the regulation of marriages, and even if the courts were to refuse to take cognizance of any amount paid in excess of the maximum. If eventually enforced, the results would be complex. First, since the large amount at present paid is a factor in stabilizing marriages, a reduction of the amount might tend to loosen the marriage bond. Secondly, the discretion of the father in fixing the amount is an acknowledgement of his authority over his daughter; if he were deprived of this discretion, it is possible that his control over his daughter would be lessened after marriage. At the present time, this would react to the woman's disadvantage; as we shall indicate shortly, the bond between a woman and her family works to protect her against her husband in case of dispute. Thirdly, it would, in one way, lessen the number of irregular marriages. Of the elopements which take place, a large number, though not a majority, occur because the husband cannot pay the *mafungu* demanded; if the amount were reduced, such cases would be rarer. Fourthly, the restriction is based on present standards of wealth; if the standards were improved the suggested amount would become little more than a formality and the restriction might thus cause difficulties in the future. Thus the setting of a maximum would have various effects, some tending to reinforce the stability of marriage and family, others to their weakening.

As a general rule, the payment of *mafungu* is necessary to legalize the marriage. Unless it has been paid, a husband cannot force a runaway wife to return to him, nor can he exact compensation for adultery. Nevertheless, elopements occur frequently, and there are many irregular marriages.[1] In some cases these soon break up. An extreme instance is that of a woman who married fifteen husbands in two or three years; not one of them had handed over the *mafungu* and they were not able to keep her. But the majority of such unions have more stability. They are recognized by the community; and if they last long enough, they are considered as differing in no way from other marriages. Nevertheless, they occupy an anomalous legal position. In the case of a quarrel, neither has any rights over the other, and the union can be dissolved at the will of either.

[1] e.g. twelve out of sixty-two marriages in a portion of the Tanangozi area were runaway marriages, and no *mafungu* was paid.

The payment of *mafungu* to legitimize the children is not necessary among the Hehe. Whether or not the mother is married to the physical father, the latter can claim the child as his own; the child enjoys full social rights and there is no stigma attached to his birth. Unless evidence to the contrary is produced, a child is presumed to be the son of his mother's husband. But various kinds of evidence will be accepted to prove physical paternity; and, if the physical father wishes to prove his paternity and thus to become the socially recognized father, it is not a difficult matter. If the mother is the wife of another man, he must, of course, pay the adultery compensation, and he must pay an extra bull as compensation for the nurture of the child. But the husband of the mother has no claim on the child unless he is the physical father, and the payment of *mafungu* only establishes marriage, not social paternity.[1]

Marriage usually follows betrothal after an interval of one or two months. At this ceremony, disputes between the two families are again settled, the members of the woman's family still constituting themselves the judges. The *mafungu* is paid over; or, if the husband has failed to pay the full amount, agreements are made to accept a lesser amount, arrangements are made for future delivery, or the wedding is postponed until the whole amount is paid. This latter contingency seldom occurs. For the remainder of the cere-

---

[1] Cf. G. Gordon Brown, 'Legitimacy and Paternity amongst the Hehe', *American Journal of Sociology*, vol. xxxviii, no. 2, Sept. 1932.

mony, which lasts from noon until far into the night, the groom's intermediaries make repeated requests to the father to hand over the bride. When this is done, the marriage is legally complete and the bride is taken to the groom's home. A number of factors may alter the details of the ceremony, but these are its essential aspects.

The marriage ceremonies and the transactions associated with them emphasize several points. Firstly, the woman passes from the home of her family to that of her husband. Secondly, it is to the advantage of the husband that he secure the wife, hence he must pay the *mafungu* to secure the stability of the marriage. Thirdly, the wife's family assert their authority throughout, and the fact of marriage does not mean that they relinquish their function as the protectors of the woman.

The wife normally goes to the home of her husband. This does not necessarily imply a place distant from her own family. While it is the right of the husband to take his wife to whatever home he will, yet the wife's family will not readily consent to marriage with a man whose home is distant; and it is sometimes made a condition of marriage that the wife's home be built near that of her parents.

The manner in which the question of residence is settled is a good example both of the formal status of husband and wife, and of how the relationship works out in practice. Strictly speaking, the woman occupies a status inferior to that of her husband. She must live where he decides; she must ask his permission to leave home, for example, to visit her relatives; and she must obey his orders in the care of the children. In actual fact, none of these demands can be enforced to any extreme degree by the husband. The woman's character will often give her a position of superiority; and, behind her, there is always the power of her united family, who will see that she obtains not only her legal rights but many extra concessions. In law, a woman occupies an inferior status, but her rights within that status are absolute; in practice, she is in an even better position than law and custom, formally interpreted, would allow her.

The obligations assumed by husband and wife provide for the regulation of sexual intercourse, the reproduction and nurture of children, the establishment of an approved form of social life, and a system of economic co-operation.

The husband has an exclusive right to sexual intercourse with his wife. Under certain restrictions, which allow for menstruation, pregnancy, and the period of lactation, she cannot refuse him this privilege; and she must refuse it to every one else. If she commits adultery, he has a right to material compensation from her and from the adulterer. In return, she has the right to the sexual attentions of her husband, and his failure to give them constitutes a valid ground for divorce. But she has not an exclusive claim to these attentions. A polygynist has other wives; and a wife has no legal grounds for complaint, even if her husband lies with a woman to whom he is not married. From the point of view of the man, the only restraints upon illicit sexual relations are the liability to pay damages if he lies with the wife of another and the difficulty of seducing unmarried women.

The woman believes that it is the duty of her husband to provide her with children. If pregnancy does not immediately follow marriage, or if it does not follow shortly after the weaning of a previous child, it is the duty of the husband to seek fertility medicine. If he fails in this, he can be ordered to do so by the courts; and continued failure will lead to divorce. Both husband and wife desire children, but the wife is considered to have the greater cause for complaint if the union is infertile. After birth, each partner may demand the appropriate services from the other as regards the proper care of the child. The father must provide shelter and the necessary medicines and must take an active interest generally in its upbringing. The mother must care for it properly and give it the food considered necessary. She is also responsible for its early training. Each parent must perform the duties sanctioned by custom, otherwise the child will suffer.

Marriage is considered the normal state of all adults and is a necessary condition to a satisfactory and dignified life. This end is promoted by a mass of rules governing social contacts. Each sex lives to some extent apart from the other, men eating in the company of men, women with women. Each sex must be assisted, or at least not frustrated, by the other in the pursuit of a satisfactory mode of association with other members of the community. A wife cannot unreasonably be prevented from visiting her kindred; she has a right to the society of other women of the neighbourhood; but she has not the right of conversing with other men in situations where improprieties are possible. The husband is freer than his wife. There is no restraint on his actions by his wife, except the negative one that he must not allow other occupations to prevent him from fulfilling his specific obligations to her.

The economic co-operation of marriage involves some division of labour and some labour in common. Both sexes cultivate the soil, but the woman does more than the man. Upon the woman falls most of the regular household routine—cooking, carrying water, bringing in firewood, and keeping the house in order. To the man falls the care of the cattle, the cutting of firewood, and the task of house-building. If either husband or wife fails to perform these duties as regulated by custom, the other has a right to be aggrieved; and continual neglect of some important economic function will cause dissolution of the marriage.

Until now, we have considered the relationship between one husband and one wife. But among the Hehe polygyny is widespread. It is not confined to men of wealth or position, and, to understand marriage as a whole, it is necessary to appreciate the nature of the polygynous group.

A few figures will indicate the extent to which it is practised. As a sample, the taxpayers of thirteen headmen, representing all sections of the tribe, are taken.[1] In the communities administered by these headmen, there are 4,054 taxpayers. The numbers of the wives are as follows:

Unmarried men	. .	1,026, or 25·3 per cent.
Men with 1 wife	. .	1,881, ,, 46·4 ,,
,, ,, 2 wives	. .	838, ,, 20·7 ,,
,, ,, 3 ,,	. .	211, ,, 5·2 ,,
,, ,, 4 ,,	. .	62, ,, 1·5 ,,
,, ,, 5 ,,	. .	24 ⎫
,, ,, 6 ,,	. .	6 ⎬ together 0·9 per cent.
,, ,, 7 ,,	. .	4 ⎪
,, ,, 9 ,,	. .	2 ⎭

Some other facts of significance emerge. 28·3 per cent. of the men have more than 1 wife; and, if married men are considered by themselves, 38 per cent. of them have more than 1 wife. The figures also show that for every 100 married men there are, on the average, 153 married women.

The mathematical possibility of polygyny as a widespread social condition depends upon two factors, the

[1] These figures are compiled from the tax assessment rolls, 1933. The plural wives' tax was introduced into the tribe in 1932, and the number of wives of each taxpayer had thus to be recorded. Independent inquiries in limited areas give results which coincide with the assessment rolls to within 5 per cent. The 4,054 sample is about 22 per cent. of the total number of taxpayers in the tribe.

excess of women over men and the earlier marriage of the women. (*a*) The census[1] shows that the ratio of females to males in the tribe is 6 to 5; (*b*) the figures tabulated above show that 25 per cent. of men in the tribe are unmarried. The vast majority of these are youths aged from 16 to 21 or 22. Women of the same ages are nearly always married. Women have thus a longer period of married life than men, and, if we assume that men and women have the same average length of life, the ratio of women's married life to men's is demonstrated to be 4 to 3. Multiplying these two ratios together, we have $\frac{6}{5} \times \frac{4}{3} = \frac{24}{15}$. There is thus a possibility of 160 married women for every 100 married men. This possibility corresponds fairly closely with the fact that there are 153 married women for every 100 married men.

When a man has more than one wife, he owes to each wife the same obligations as the monogamist; and each wife owes the same obligations to her husband as would be the case if she were the only wife. Each wife is entitled to her fair share of her husband's sexual attentions; the ordinary arrangement is for the husband to visit his wives in rotation. If any wife is forbidden sexual intercourse—if, for example, she is suckling a child—the husband must still visit her in her turn and eat the food she has cooked, even though he sleeps with another.

Each wife is also entitled to demand children; when her previous child is weaned, she must receive

[1] The Native Census, 1931.

the medicines believed necessary for conception. Each wife must receive and give the same social consideration; but here there is difference. The first wife has a special position. She is the *munya kaye*, the possessor of the house. This title does not confer any marital or material privileges; she must bear her share of the labour of agriculture and must share her husband's attentions equally, but it does give her a social esteem above that enjoyed by her co-wives. In addition, if the husband occupies a hereditary office, her eldest son has the first right of succession. Nowadays, this right is only nominal. In practice, either the eldest son, whoever his mother, succeeds, or, in place of him, the most able son is given the post. But the Hehe belief that the son of the *munya kaye* should succeed is a recognition of the social pre-eminence of the first wife, even though this position confers no real privileges. In economic matters, each wife must receive equal attention. The husband assists each in the cultivation of her plantation by an equitable subdivision of his land and by performing certain tasks; he provides housing for each; and he pays equal attention to all his children.

Polygyny does not thus imply the setting up of a large joint household, but the creation of a series of individual households, the common factor being the husband. In the matter of housing, each wife has, ideally, two rooms; she must never be without at least one room of her own. This is sometimes done by building a large house in which each wife has her quarters, sometimes by building separate houses, and sometimes, if a man has a large number of wives, by dividing them into two or more groups, each group having a joint house, but each wife with her own quarters within the house. If a man fails to provide a wife with her house, she has cause for divorce; therefore the obligation to build is no small one for the successful polygynist.

Although each wife sets up a separate household, yet in many cases there is a good deal of co-operation. Co-wives owe to each other certain services which they cannot avoid. They must render mutual assistance at difficult tasks, such as the cooking of beer; they owe certain attentions to each other, in case of illness; and no one must try to exact from her husband more than her fair share of privileges. In addition, there is often a large measure of voluntary co-operation; many tasks are shared, as, for example, the care of the children. But this does not necessarily occur, and a wife has no claim against her co-wife as long as the formal obligations are fulfilled.

The successful polygynist is the man who is able to maintain all mutual obligations, both between himself and his wives and between the wives themselves. It is essential that he be fair and impartial. He must not favour one wife at the expense of the others. If a quarrel arises between two wives, he seldom judges it himself, but calls in an arbitrator. If he did judge the case himself, he would almost inevitably be accused of partiality. The husband must, in short, exercise continual tact as well as firmness. If he shows himself capable of keeping peace, he will be able to add to his wives; if he fails to do so, he will lose even those whom he has.

To be a successful polygynist is thus no easy task; but in Hehe eyes the reward is worth the trouble. To have a plurality of wives increases the probability of offspring, always desired by both men and women; it adds to the social esteem in which he is held; he is able to extend hospitality on a larger scale than the man with only one wife; and, if his wives are numerous enough, he can escape the drudgery of agriculture.

Under present conditions, polygyny serves many useful social ends. It provides a recognized status for all surplus women. It is a traditionally accepted manner of improving the individual standard of living, among a people who have no means of adding to wealth by capital investment. And it sets free a certain number of men to perform public duties. When polygyny dies out, as it may, it is to be hoped that other means of satisfying these needs will be developed.

At the same time, polygyny is not to be regarded with unqualified approval. It develops evils of its own. The status of women will undergo little fundamental change as long as it lasts; and, as for the men, it removes a certain amount of stimulus to improve the standard of living by more effective economic activities. Moreover, personal relationships are not satisfactory. While many women settle down amicably in a polygynous household and enjoy the fact that some of their tasks are lightened by the presence of co-wives, yet quarrels arising from jealousy often occur, and divorce is more frequent than in the case of monogamous marriages. In addition, it is not conducive to sexual morality: a large majority of Hehe women commit adultery, but the wives of polygynists are the worst offenders. This is a constant threat to family stability, the basis of Hehe life. In short, polygyny, while a present social necessity, is not an entirely satisfactory institution; but it should not be destroyed until other institutions have been developed to perform its present functions.

It has been already suggested that marriage not only involves the relationship between man and wife, but that two groups are concerned, the families of each. Marriage is individual, but it creates a bond between two previously unrelated groups. This follows because the husband still owes obligations to his own kindred and the wife still remains a member of her own family. A mass of observances exist to regulate this new relationship, which can only be summarized here. Husband and wife must each pay a ceremonious respect to the parents and elders of the family of the other. This prevents unseemly and socially disintegrating quarrels. On the other hand, the relationship between relatives by marriage in the same generation is easy and familiar. It sometimes leads to a man marrying his wife's sister; the bond is already created, and it therefore requires less adjustment to marry

THE HEHE TRIBE

again into the same family. It also leads to what might be called preferred adultery. A man is more apt to commit adultery with his wife's sister or with his brother's wife than with other women. The familiarity exists by reason of the relationship. The incest bar is absent, and it is an easy step to sexual intimacy. It is still, however, adultery: adulterer and adulteress must pay the full compensation if caught.

The existence of this bond created by marriage finds recognition in the custom of inheritance of wives. If a man dies, his brothers, sons, or close relatives inherit his wives. If a wife dies, the husband has a claim on her family for another wife. In either case, no further *mafungu* is paid. The basis of this custom is not that marriage is a group marriage, but that the secondary bonds created by marriage are maintained by a further marriage. It has already been mentioned that this custom is dying out, and that if a woman objects to being inherited she gets a divorce automatically. This change in custom has caused the evolution of new laws. If a man dies and his wife refuses to be inherited, the question arises as to the repayment of the *mafungu*. The courts now rule that if the woman has borne no children, the *mafungu* must be returned; if she has one child, part of the *mafungu* must be returned; and if she has borne two or more children, nothing is returned.

Marriage may be dissolved for a number of reasons. The man and the woman do not have equal rights in this respect. A man may divorce his wife without reason; a woman must have good grounds for doing so. The reason for this inequality is partly the superior status of the husband and partly because of polygyny. It is in the interest of the man to have as many wives as he can; if one does not suit him, he can always hope to get another. A woman, on the other hand, has only one husband; and if she cannot agree with him, she must get a divorce before she marries another.

Most suits for divorce are initiated by the wife. The cause given is nearly always illtreatment or failure on the part of the husband to fulfil his obligations to her. He may be accused of denying her sexual intercourse; of neglect to seek medicines for fertility or for illness; of not providing her with a house; or of general neglect or desertion. These or similar accusations, if substantiated, will be accepted as sufficient by the courts and she will obtain her divorce.

Sometimes a woman will claim a divorce on the ground that she does not love her husband. This is not considered sufficient ground by the courts, and the woman is always told to return to her husband. Nevertheless, if a woman persists, she can always get a divorce for this reason in the end. She will fail once or twice, but, if she persistently refuses to return, either her husband will agree to the divorce or the courts will take it upon themselves to dissolve the marriage.

When divorce is granted, the *mafungu* must be returned to the husband by the woman's father or brother. If the cause is illtreatment resulting in serious injury, the court may order that a part or the whole of it be retained as compensation. If the woman has borne her husband children, the husband may refuse to receive back the *mafungu*. This, however, is an act of grace on his part. If the woman insists on leaving her husband without good cause, she must pay compensation in addition to returning the *mafungu*.

We have given more space to marriage than to kinship because matrimonial disputes give rise to a large proportion of the litigation which occurs in the tribe. Marriage is a difficult relationship: the mutual obligations involved call for a large part of the attention and energy of both man and wife, and failures to fulfil them are frequent. When these difficulties are accentuated by polygyny, when jealousy causes bitterness and discord, and when many women feel themselves aggrieved by neglect, quarrels are still more apt to occur. It is consequently of some importance to understand the circumstances giving rise to such disagreements.

(*c*) *The Public Regulation of Family Life.*

The organization of kinship and marriage involves a multitude of reciprocal obligations. These obligations are, of course, subject to much variation, in accordance with character and circumstance. The Hehe social organization is flexible enough to allow for a considerable variation within limits; but, once these limits are passed, once obligations are so minimized or so distorted as to cause a serious departure from accepted social norms, they must be readjusted.

Disputes arising within the family or matrimonial disputes are, if serious enough, taken to the headman or to the sub-chief for settlement. But disputes may also be settled within the family, by a family council. These disputes are generally petty; but the action of the family council is frequently effective in preventing them from becoming serious quarrels and in preventing small grudges from growing into permanent estrangements.

The family council usually consists of the effective senior men who are resident within the community. There is no regular appointment; all who wish may take part, if they have a recognized ability in the settlement of disputes. If the case is serious enough, kindred may be summoned from a distance to participate.

Matrimonial disputes are frequently settled by the wife's family. She feels aggrieved at some wrong and takes refuge with her parents. She states the case to her father and kindred. If they consider that it has no foundation or that it is petty, they advise her to return to her husband. If it is a serious accusation, they advise her to go to the headman. Such advice is, in a sense, a judicial decision. It is made after a deliberate discussion by responsible men. That these men have a bias in favour of the plaintiff makes it all the more impressive if a decision is given against her.

Disputes of a different nature are also settled in this

way. A man once went to the house of his father-in-law and discovered that the latter had stolen his spear. The nature of the relationship between father-in-law and son-in-law made a direct accusation difficult. The son-in-law took a friend with him, pointed to the spear, and asked whose it was. The friend confirmed the ownership. Thus supported, the son-in-law brought the matter up the next time the family was assembled. The father-in-law admitted the theft and offered to return the spear and to pay compensation. The son-in-law accepted the spear, but refused compensation.

Occasionally the family council tries more serious cases. A man seduced the wife of a kinsman. For various reasons, it was decided to keep the affair within the family. All officials were rigidly excluded from the council, even some petty headmen who, on the basis of kinship, would ordinarily have attended. The offender was judged to pay ten shillings compensation. Had the case gone to court, the penalty would have been much greater.

These few examples must suffice to show how disputes are settled. The family council also performs other functions. It occasionally settles matters of family policy, and it regulates transactions of a ceremonial and legal nature.

The Kihwele family has already been mentioned.[1] They were vested as a group with one of the petty headmanships under the headman of Wasa. In 1930

[1] See above, p. 77.

they had a series of quarrels with the headman. After a time, the old man called the family together, and it was decided that they should all resign. The headman protested too late; and the position was given to another family. It is not thereby suggested that the family frequently acts as a unit, but when it does so, its actions are regulated by the council.

Reference has already been made to some of the ceremonial and legal functions of the family council. At betrothal and marriage, the family of the bride form a council to settle disputes and to arrange the bride-wealth. Another characteristic legal and ceremonial assembly is the *mitangu*. In this, a religious ceremony (the breaking of mourning three months after death) is combined with a system of legal acts, the distribution of the estate of the deceased, the payment of his debts, and the collection of what is owed him.[1] The father of the deceased presides, or, if he is dead or ineffective, the senior able male of the paternal branch of the family takes charge—a brother, a classificatory brother, or the father's brother. To avoid quarrels, the local headman is invited as arbitrator, but he only decides matters referred to him and does not otherwise interfere. Custom dictates the general principles of distribution, but the family council must decide how these principles are applied. For example, valuable property, chiefly cattle and money, must go to

[1] Sometimes the religious and the legal ceremonies are performed on separate occasions. The religious ceremonies are then called *mahiliwo*, the legal acts *mitangu*.

the close kindred of the deceased. Elder sons have a preference over younger sons, sons over daughters, and children over brothers and sisters of the deceased. The family council must decide how to apply these principles to the division of, say, seventeen head of cattle among two sons, three daughters, and two brothers. Less valuable property, spears, chairs, pots, and tools, is distributed among a wider circle of kindred, the general principle being that every branch of the family must receive something. After the property is distributed, the inheritance of the dead man's wife or wives is discussed, but this is done perfunctorily nowadays, since the women will decide for themselves. The presiding elder makes most decisions, after listening to the opinions of the others; quarrels are immediately referred to the headman, and, while disagreements sometimes persist, the division of the property is usually accomplished without serious trouble.

The family council is thus both a factor regulating family life and a centre for agreement. The way in which it functions is typical of Hehe institutions. Unlimited and free discussion is allowed; grievances may be stated publicly; the whole community affected may participate; and decisions given are expressions of public opinion, regulated by well understood principles and guided by the presidency of the man who is accepted as the natural leader.

It is as a member of the family council that the Hehe acquires his legal training. He learns to argue his case, to sift evidence, and to arrange compromises. Some Hehe never learn to hold their own in public discussion and are rather despised for this reason; for, according to Hehe standards, a man who is able in settling disputes is worthy of public respect. Thus the family council is intimately related to the whole legal system of the tribe. Both as an organ for the maintenance of order and as a legal training-ground, it plays an important part in tribal life.

B. *LAW* [1]

In the previous section, we have had to refer to law-givers and judges and to indicate to some degree the nature of Hehe law. This section will therefore involve some repetition; but that is unavoidable, if the subject is to be fully understood.

Hehe law is not a code of rules, but is based upon the recognition of an existing state of society. In all social relationships, the Hehe recognize the existence of certain obligations and privileges. Thus there are the specific obligations existing between kindred, varying with the nature of the kinship bond. There are, similarly, obligations to one's superiors. Finally, there are the general obligations to other members of the community. These obligations imply the existence of certain privileges, specific as regards one's

---

[1] The writing of this section has been much assisted by reference to Professor Malinowski's *Crime and Custom in Savage Society*, and to J. H. Driberg's 'Primitive Law in Eastern Africa', *Africa*, vol. i, no. 1, pp. 63–72. Acknowledgements are also made to Professor Radcliffe-Brown for suggestions made in conversation.

kindred, general as regards the rest of the community. The nature of the kinship privileges has already been indicated. The general privileges are the right to immunity from physical harm, to the enjoyment of social life, to reputation, and to property. These rights and privileges are not abstract, they cannot be claimed from any entity known as society. They are simply the natural consequences of living in a particular form of ordered society. Law, as we have said, is the recognition of that form of ordered society. As long as there is no disturbance—as long, that is, as all obligations are fulfilled and all rights respected, so long does society function harmoniously, and there is no need for the intervention of a legal process. If, however, some obligation is not fulfilled, or if some right has been infringed, the functioning of the social mechanism is disturbed, and a process of law is necessary to restore it.

Law, however, does not take cognizance of the non-fulfilment of all obligations, and it is here that the distinction can be made between simple custom and custom enforced by law. A young man who is getting married has a right to expect certain reasonable assistance from his father to pay the *mafungu* (bride-wealth). If the father refuses to assist, the son can, in the last resort, claim it in the court; the obligation is recognized by law. If the son marries a second wife, it is customary for the father to assist him again, according to his means. But if he fails, the son cannot force him to do so in court. The obligation on the part of the father is moral, not legal; it is a custom, not a law. There is, in brief, a series of obligations; only the more socially essential are recognized in law.

If some obligation has not been fulfilled, or if some right has not been respected, there is a social disturbance. This disturbance affects society as a whole, but its cause is a specific injury to a person or a group of people. Theft, for example, is a disturbance to society; but society is disturbed because the property rights of a person or a group have been infringed. Consequently, the accuser is not the community but the individual whose property has been stolen. Similarly, adultery is a disturbance of society because a man's exclusive rights to the sexual functions of his wife have been infringed. This disturbance can only be quieted when the personal injury has been remedied; and the husband, not society, is the accuser.

An offence against the law is thus the disturbance of a system of social observances. Society as a whole is affected, but only because a person or a group is injured. As a result, society does not punish; it restores the social balance by righting the specific injuries inflicted by one individual or group upon another. Punishment does not meet the case, because, while it penalizes the offender, it confers no compensating advantage upon the offended. The Hehe method is, therefore, to order the offender to pay material compensation to the injured party. The transfer of property heals the injury and the social disturbance is quieted.

In the olden days, nearly all offences were thus dealt with, as injuries to individuals or groups. Theft necessitated the return of the stolen property, together with the payment of compensation for the violation of property rights. Assaults and violence also demanded compensation. Even murder could be compensated by payment of a large number of oxen to the family of the victim.

Since the aim of legal procedure is to restore a disturbed social balance, it is necessary that the judgement be acceptable to all parties. The offender must first admit his fault. In practice, of course, he never does, until it is proved in court. He then makes his admission, and this is considered an essential part of the legal settlement. The injured party must agree to accept the compensation. The amount is actually set by the court, but formal agreement to accept the amount named is required, before the dispute can be considered at an end. Thus both plaintiff and defendant are at least passive participants in the judgement; and a satisfactory conclusion to any case involves a general acceptance of the fact that the agreed payment will end the disturbance. This again emphasizes the conclusion made elsewhere, that the Hehe judge is not an arbitrary magistrate, but the chairman of an assembly which represents public opinion.

In Hehe law, there is no distinction between civil and criminal cases. Every offence is an injury to a person. The injured party must accordingly take steps to obtain compensation for the injury. This is done by accusing the offender before a community leader, headman, sub-chief, or chief. The leader of the community takes no action until thus appealed to. Hehe legal procedure may thus be said to be a system of cognizance of private torts.

In the olden days, there were two exceptions to this general rule. First, witchcraft was a practice so dangerous to the community as a whole that the witch or warlock must be put to death as a matter of public safety. The accusation was made to the chief. He ordered the poison ordeal (*mwafi*); and, if the signs went against the accused, he was speared. Secondly, treason was an offence against the chief. The proceedings could hardly be called legal. A man suspected of conspiring against the power of the chief was simply killed by order; he had no opportunity of defending himself in court. Death was the only punishment in Hehe law, and that only for these two offences. All other offences were against individuals, and involved the payment of compensation, not punishment.

The composition of a Hehe court has already been described. The rules of evidence are given elsewhere.[1] It only remains to suggest the procedure. The plaintiff speaks first. He is followed by the defendant. Witnesses are then brought by both sides. The discussion becomes more and more open. Each litigant has not only his witnesses, but his relatives and friends, to speak on his behalf. There is no limit to the

[1] See below, Appendix C, answer to question no. 23, pp. 255-7.

time any one may speak, nor to the number of times he speaks. There is often some stage in the proceedings when confusion reigns. Then the more responsible men, led by the judge, begin to restore order. The essential facts are emphasized. Interruptions are firmly quelled. The evidence is reviewed; and if the case is concluded satisfactorily, the defendant admits his fault, compensation is awarded, the plaintiff agrees, and the case is ended. On the whole, the proceedings are animated but orderly. Every one has his full say and is satisfied. If the judgement is not satisfactory, the argument is begun over again. If the court, as usual, remains firm, the disgruntled litigant either agrees or announces his intention of appealing. If he persists, the case goes to a higher court; but often it is a last protest; and, when it proves unavailing, he pays the compensation ordered.

The principles and procedure of Hehe law may be illustrated by an account of how the offence of *maligo* is dealt with. *Maligo* (Swahili *matusi*) consists of hurling abusive epithets at another or of making obscene or objectionable statements about another. It is thus *maligo* to call another person a witch or warlock, to make obscene statements about his parents, or to accuse him of offences for which no proof can be offered. There is no exact equivalent for it in English, the nearest word being slander. It is a serious offence in Hehe opinion. It publicly humiliates the slandered person and lowers him in his own estimation and in the estimation of those who hear what is said. It violates his right to social esteem and reputation. If the slandered person is a kinsman, the offence is even worse: the mutual respect which is necessary to the maintenance of kinship bonds is destroyed, and Hehe social life is thus threatened at its foundations. The offence is of greater or less gravity according to the nature of the epithets used and to the sex and position of the person slandered. If the offender is a man, it is worse to slander a woman than a person of his own sex; worse to slander a member of the ascendant generation than one of his own; and worst of all to slander a person to whom he must observe a ceremonial respect, his paternal aunt or his mother-in-law. If the injured party brings an action, all the circumstances are discussed in full: the conditions giving rise to the outburst, the relationship between the parties, the epithets used, and any alleviating or aggravating factors. Generally, the culprit is willing to admit his fault; compensation is assessed in accordance with all the attendant circumstances; and peace is thus restored. In a small community, the violent emotions arising from such an offence cannot be disregarded. If given no outlet, they constitute a continual threat to social stability and must be dealt with as seriously as any other offence causing profound feelings of injury.

The principles of Hehe law are best exemplified, in these days, in the headmen's courts. Since they have no power of fining or of imprisoning, they can only order the payment of compensation, and, allowing for changed social circumstances, they probably give judgements in much the same manner as their predecessors did. The officially recognized courts of the chief and the sub-chiefs are in a different position. Having the power to fine or imprison, they feel themselves to be magistrates in the European sense; and, while the cases they deal with mostly arise from native custom and are treated from that point of view, yet European principles of punishment are often introduced[1] as well as, or even in place of, compensation. This will be discussed more fully in the following chapter; here, it is merely necessary to indicate that native law is ceasing to be pure and is undergoing change as the result of contact with European legal concepts.

C. *LAND TENURE*

The Hehe system of land tenure is not a complex one. The reason for this is that there is more than enough arable land in the tribe, and the individual can always find land in any area in which he wants to live. The population of the tribe is approximately 87,000; the tribal area is about 12,000 square miles. Of this, alienations amount to about 365 square miles; and a considerable proportion of the remainder is not arable. But even if only half of the total area is available for native needs, it is still far in excess of what is required.

The individual receives his grant of land originally from the headman. The right to sufficient land for

[1] Too often, in the opinion of the anthropologist.

cultivation goes with the right of residence. Thus, if a new-comer receives permission from the headman to reside in the community, he selects a plot. He then notifies the headman, and the latter, or a delegated *mkalani*, examines the land, makes sure that no previous rights are infringed, and confirms the right to cultivate. The new-comer then has a good title to the land he has selected.

The grant of land is an easy matter if the new-comer settles at some little distance from the nearest existing house. He will usually cultivate the area around or near his house, and new ground for natural expansion and rotation of crops will be readily available. If, however, he settles next to some one who has already broken ground for cultivation, care must be taken that there is no possibility of overlapping. To avoid this possibility, a definite boundary is fixed. This may be a natural object, such as a tree or a stone, or, failing a natural boundary, a line is cut with a hoe between the two plots. One man may then expand in one direction, the other man in the other.

When a large number of people live comparatively close to each other, land tenure becomes more complex. Each person has a plot of land around his house, but this is generally insufficient, and a further allocation of land must be made. It often happens that one large area of land in the neighbourhood is more suitable for agriculture than another; this is divided among all who live near by. It is not, however, divided into large plots, each plot being assigned to one man; it is divided into strips. One man may have several strips, but they are not all adjacent; they will be scattered among strips owned by other men. For example, A will own strips numbered consecutively 1, 5, 7, 8, and 11; and B will own strips 2, 6, 9, 12, and 14; the result is that no one man has all the best land, the good land being divided with approximate equality amongst every one concerned.

For the cultivation of the staple crops, land may thus be owned in one large plot, if the house is at a distance from other houses; or it may be owned in strips, if the owner has close neighbours. In addition to land possessed in this manner, there are plots for other purposes. There are the eleusine plantations, the root-crop plantations, and the dry-weather plantations.

The cultivation of eleusine (which is used for brewing beer) differs from ordinary cultivation. The eleusine plantations (*mahonyo*) are small and are fertilized by ash obtained from trees cut and burnt on the spot. They must thus be made in wooded country and are only available for one year, since, in the following year, other uncut bush must be sought. The man selects two or three suitable areas, none of them large, makes a mark, such as a cut on a tree, and that bush is his for the year. There is usually enough bush land for the whole population; and we have never been in an area where disputes arose over this temporary right of cultivation. After the harvest, ownership lapses.

Root crops, consisting of sweet potatoes (*fingamba*) and cassava (*mihogo*), may be grown in the ordinary plantations, but it is common to plant them separately. The land for these crops is selected and granted in accordance with the same procedure as that followed in the case of ordinary plantations.

Besides the large annual planting, small plantations are made during the dry season on the banks of rivers, where the crops can be irrigated. These plantations (*fyungu*) are granted separately. In many areas, river lands are scarce, and the grants are small and cannot always be given to every one. The title continues from year to year, and, if a new-comer arrives in the community, he must sometimes do without *fyungu* until an older occupant moves away and his ownership lapses.

Except in the case of the eleusine plantations, which are only used for one year, the plantations are the property of the occupant for as long as the occupation is effective. The criteria of effective occupation are two. The first is residence. The lands granted near the house remain the property of the man to whom they were granted, as long as he lives in the neighbourhood. He may not always cultivate them, but no one else may do so; they are his until he moves away or until he voluntarily surrenders his title to the headman. This is obviously the case where a man's lands are in a solid block around his house; it also applies where ownership is in strips, so long as the owner does not move to a distance.

The other criterion of effective occupation is continuous cultivation. The plantations for root-crops, often at a distance from the house, only remain the property of the cultivator so long as he uses them. If he lets a year (that is, a complete planting season) pass without cultivation, any one else may plant crops there; and if the headman confirms the title, the land becomes his. Continuous cultivation is also necessary to retain ownership of the dry-weather plantations. Sometimes, also, a man will wish to retain his plantations after he has moved to another community. He may be slow in breaking new ground, and therefore wish to utilize the old land until his new plantations are ready. As long as he plants his crops, the old plantations are his; but if he misses a year, they lapse to the headman, who can grant them to some one else.

Ownership of land is thus really only a right of occupancy, valid as long as the occupancy is effective; and the effectiveness is judged by residence and use in cultivation. Consequently land so possessed is not private property in the European sense of the term. It is private in that only one person can use it; it is not private in that its possession is not absolute; possession is contingent only. It is neither heritable nor saleable. It is not heritable, because, if a man's children are grown up, they will have lands of their own; and if they are young they will go to other guardians. A man's widows will be allowed to go on cultivating; but they will eventually remarry, go to their children, or be inherited. It is not saleable, first because no one will buy what is free, and secondly because ownership can only be transferred to the headman. Land is not, in itself, valuable; it is only occupation which makes it so.

While land is not transferable property, standing or growing crops are in a different category. They are the property of the person who cultivated them, subject to his social obligations. Crops are thus both saleable and heritable; but, once harvested, they have no effect on the ownership of the land.

Grazing rights are common and undefined. Cattle may graze where they will, provided they do not damage standing crops. Here, again, the problem is simple, because land is plentiful and there are only 120,000 cattle owned by the tribe, about 10 per square mile; and there has hitherto been no necessity for restriction or regulation.

The rules stated are those regulating the occupation of land by the man, the head of the household. Within the family, there are rights in land. A man must subdivide his land so that his wives and his children have plots of their own. If he does not do this, in the case of his wives at least, he can be forced to do so by the courts. Once he has granted land to a wife, it is hers as long as the marriage continues. If he takes a strip from her to give to another wife, she can claim ownership. Intra-family disputes over land-ownership are not uncommon. Frequently they are settled by the family council; but if a woman is dissatisfied with the verdict she can always claim her rights in court. Within the family, land is usually allocated in strips, the wife receiving a certain number of them, a few being allocated to the children, and the husband retaining the remainder to cultivate himself.

The system here described holds for most of the tribe. In Dabaga and Mufindi, where shifting cultivation is the rule, the same principles hold, but they are modified by the fact that ownership lapses every three or four years and new land must be granted. We have not seen the workings of the system in detail, so cannot describe it as fully as we should like.

These rules of land ownership work satisfactorily because, as noted, land is plentiful, and also because, under present conditions, there are no permanent improvements. As soon as one or other of these factors changes, the land laws must change. An examination of all the court books reveals only one case to indicate how Hehe land law, unaided by guidance from European legislation, might develop. In a dispute over land, the defendant claimed that the plaintiff had not cultivated the plot for five years. The plaintiff said that he had planted a certain number of mango trees on it. The sub-chief divided the land. To the original owner, the plaintiff, he gave the half which contained the mango trees; to the defendant, he gave the other half. He thus recognized the existence of a permanent improvement and the fact that new conditions could change the application of the customary principles. But this was an isolated judgement, and it is quite possible that a radical change in the conditions of agriculture, or in the availability of land, would necessitate radical alterations in the Hehe rules of land tenure.

D. ECONOMICS

For convenience of analysis, the economic activities of the Hehe may be divided into three groups. The first group includes all the fundamental activities necessary to the maintenance of the traditional tribal life. Of these, the most important is the cultivation of the soil, others being the care of live stock and house-building. These pursuits are fundamental, not only because they are essential to the preservation of life and health, but because they are followed by practically all members of the tribe, including those who spend part of their time at other tasks. The second group comprises the practice of the traditional crafts—smithing, woodwork, pottery, and basketwork. The third group includes all activities associated with the acquisition of money and the satisfaction of needs through the expenditure of money. These groups of economic activities are not, of course, independent of each other, but they are sufficiently distinct to permit this tentative classification.

Before discussing the Hehe system of agriculture, it must be noted that it is only in recent years that there has been any effective stimulus to the production of crops surplus to household requirements. Before European occupation, there was nothing to be done with surplus crops except to let them rot; the most industrious cultivator could ask no more than an ample food supply and sufficient extra to enable him to dispense generous hospitality. Since European occupation, there has been a slowly growing market for foodstuffs; but even to-day the market is limited, and the growing of crops for sale is decidedly a secondary consideration. Agriculture is undertaken primarily to feed the household.

In selecting a plot for cultivation, two considerations operate. The first is social: the Hehe prefer to settle in an area where they can enjoy a satisfactory social life. They must belong to a community, and preferably a community in which they have kinsmen. The second consideration is agricultural: the land must be fertile, or, at worst, it must not fall below some minimum level of fertility. The social desires can be satisfied by any one of a large variety of conditions of residence; and the need for fertile land still leaves a wide range of choice. Other factors are also taken into account; for example, water must be near and firewood available.

When the area for cultivation is once selected, the ground is broken. This task is generally performed by the man and is done after the rains. This is the hardest agricultural task and takes a long time to accomplish, the work being sometimes spread over a period of two years. During the period of breaking new ground, the family live on the produce of their old plantations. When sufficient ground has been broken, the family move to their new place of residence and begin the hoeing and planting at the beginning of the heavy rains.

Within the elementary family, there is a certain amount of common work and also some division of labour. The man, as noted, breaks the new ground. This is an annual task. It is particularly exacting when residence is being changed; but even after settlement some new ground is broken each year to take the place of plantations abandoned or left fallow.

In the annual hoeing and planting, the work is done by both sexes, but the woman does more than the man. The family plantation is divided into strips (*migunda*), some belonging to the husband, a larger number to the wife or wives. The strips of each person are not in a block, but are scattered to ensure a fair division of the more fertile land, an important factor in a polygynous household. These strips are long and narrow. They vary considerably in size and shape, from 4 to 10 yards wide and from 50 to 200 yards long. There is no uniform method of measuring the area under cultivation; a man will merely state that he has so many *migunda*, of which he cultivates a specified number, his wife or wives the remainder. Generally speaking, a man will cultivate a third of the *migunda*, a wife two-thirds. If a man has more than one wife, he will cultivate less; if he has four or five wives, he will not cultivate any.

The actual area cultivated varies greatly. Some people are known to be industrious agriculturists, others cultivate a bare minimum, and a few run short of food regularly every year. It has been estimated that, in a soil of average fertility, a man with one wife and three children should cultivate about $3\frac{1}{2}$ acres to provide food, seed, and a surplus for sale.[1] A limited number of measurements indicate that there is a considerable variation and that the above estimate may be on the low side, although some people will not cultivate even this amount. The following samples may indicate the variation.

(i) One man with two wives and three children cultivated about $5\frac{1}{2}$ acres. According to the estimate, his minimum requirements were about 4·2 acres. Of this, the man himself cultivated slightly over three-quarters of an acre, one wife cultivated about 3 acres, and the other wife cultivated $1\frac{2}{3}$ acres.

(ii) Another man, with one wife and five children, cultivated 6 acres. His minimum requirements necessitated slightly under 5 acres.

(iii) A third man, with two wives and eight children, cultivated just under 6 acres. His minimum requirements necessitated $7\frac{1}{2}$ acres. This family lives on short rations every year for two or three months before the harvest.

The staple crop is maize; subsidiary crops are eleusine, sweet potatoes, beans, ground-nuts, marrow, and, occasionally, onions and tomatoes. In the last few years, cassava has been planted because of the menace of locusts. The measurements we have made are not

---

[1] This estimate was made by Mr. C. J. MacGregor, District Agricultural Officer, Iringa, to whom acknowledgements are made.

sufficient to generalize with any certainty about the relative acreages of each crop, but we believe the following sample to be fairly representative.

On a plantation of 5½ acres, the percentage of each crop was as follows:

Maize	75 per cent.
Potatoes	17 ,,
Cassava	5 ,,
Eleusine	3 ,,

Beans and marrow were not measured separately, as they were planted along with the maize. Ground-nuts were not grown.

All cultivation is done with the hoe (*ligimilo*). The ground is first roughly broken at the end of the rains (April and May). With the new rains (late in December or early in January) the ground is hoed into a series of ridges or beds (*lugeleka, ngeleka*) and planted. For sweet potatoes, the beds are wider and higher than for maize. The eleusine is planted differently. It is either a first crop on newly-broken ground, or it is grown on special plots (*mahonyo*). To make these plots, trees are cut and burnt, since eleusine needs potash. When the rains begin, the ash is mixed with the superficial soil by means of a light hoeing and the seed is planted broadcast.

On newly-broken ground, eleusine or potatoes are sown. The second year, the crops are maize and beans, planted alternately. The third and succeeding years, maize is planted alone. The soil is generally exhausted in six or eight years, but we have seen plots cultivated regularly for more than ten years. Cattle-dung is sometimes used to manure the exhausted ground; in some areas this is the general custom, in others it is the exception. Plots which must be abandoned as unproductive are replaced by newly-broken soil. As a man's plantations become worked out, he goes farther afield to seek fertile ground; and eventually, as the plantations get farther and farther from his house, he moves his house to be near them. This system would have to be modified very considerably, if land were not so plentiful.

In addition to the main crop, planted in January, the people in some areas cultivate dry-weather plantations. These are planted on the banks of small rivers and are irrigated by furrows connecting them with the stream. They are planted in September or October, and form a welcome addition to the food-supply at a time when food is becoming scarce, before the main harvest. These plantations are small, seldom exceeding a fifth of an acre and generally only about a tenth of an acre in extent. Maize, beans, and marrow are sown. Not all Hehe possess dry-weather plantations. In some areas, only a limited amount of suitable land is available, in others there are no streams.

The foregoing account of agricultural methods applies only to the central and possibly to the southern part of the tribe. We have made no systematic or detailed observations in the north-eastern area, where millet is the main crop; in the north, where rice is grown; or in the east and south-east in the forest areas, where shifting agriculture, based on the burning of forest for fertilization, is the rule. As the central and southern parts are more heavily populated than the other areas, the foregoing account is descriptive of the agricultural methods of 40 per cent. of the tribe.

The cultivation of the individual plantations is performed by means of both individual and co-operative labour. Thus a man or a woman will spend a good many days working alone on his or her plantations. In addition, a man must give some days to helping his wife, and she some days to helping him. A polygynist must give the same amount of assistance to each wife. Besides this co-operation within the family, there is a limited amount of community co-operation. A man lets it be known that on a certain day his wife will have cooked native beer (*ugimbi*) for those who help him with his hoeing, and he invites relatives and neighbours to come. The work is done in the morning; at noon a pot of beer is brought to the fields, and, when this is consumed, the work continues until two or three o'clock. The people assembled then retire to the house and finish the beer. The beer is in a sense a reward for labour, but it is the strength of the social obligation that causes one man to assist his fellow. The social compulsion varies. A close kinsman must assist; and a near neighbour or a close friend generally does so. More distant kinsmen may or may not assist. Acquaintances living two to four hours away may come if there is nothing else to do. It is noteworthy that a visitor will be given beer to drink even if he has done no work; and in any community there are a number of men who regularly attend whenever beer is provided, but who seldom do any work. Thus co-operative work on individual plantations is accomplished by means of reciprocal obligations of assistance. Custom decrees that beer must be provided, but the beer is definitely an act of hospitality, not a payment.

Though any individual may not thus summon the community to assist him for more than a day at a time, he may summon more than one cultivation-party during the process of planting. A man may ask for help to cultivate his maize plantations, his potato gardens, and his eleusine; and each wife may summon assistance for her own gardens. The consequence is that, during the heavy planting season, there is a succession of working-parties.

The Hehe system of co-operation in cultivation does not result in any material gain; in fact, it increases the amount of work required. Every man who gives assistance on the days of co-operation must be assisted in his turn; and the work given and received cancel each other in the long run. In addition, beer must be provided, and the process of preparing beer lasts five days. When it is remembered that beer must be dispensed to all comers, whether they work or not, it is obvious that the whole system of hospitality in return for work merely adds to the required labour during a very busy period. But, though there are no material gains, this traditional method has very real advantages. The task of cultivating with the hoe is long and dreary. One man can break only a limited amount of ground in a day, and the work, if done entirely alone, may seem endless. The co-operation of a group changes drudgery into a social event; it provides a social stimulus to effort; and the visible results of one day's co-operative effort are a sufficient recompense for the trouble involved.

After the crops are sown, they must be weeded once or twice. This task falls to the woman, both on her own plots and on her husband's. The harvesting, which occurs in July, is also done by the women, each working individually.

When harvested, the crops are first dried and then put into food stores (*chimba* or *kisande*). Each individual has his or her own store. The husband has the right to dispose of his store as he pleases; he may sell it or make presents to his kindred, particularly his sister or parents, if they are in danger of scarcity. If the number of a man's wives frees him from the labour of cultivating his own gardens, he still has his own stores, formed by the contributions of his wives. The stores of the women are not so completely their own property. They must supply the household needs first; and, even if there is an unusually good harvest, and consequently a large surplus, they cannot dispose of any foodstuffs without the husband's consent; and the proceeds are usually shared with him. The man has complete ownership of his individual crops; the woman owns her crops jointly with her husband.

Children possess their own strips from the time they are about 12 years old. An unmarried boy, living with his parents, owns his own crop, but he generally presents his father with a portion of it for distribution among his wives. An unmarried girl gives most of her crop to her own mother, retaining a small quantity to dispose of as she wishes.

The agricultural activities of the tribe involve a great deal of co-operation between the sexes; some tasks are shared, some are divided, but both sexes contribute, though unequally, to the production of the food-supply. In other activities, the division of labour is more marked.

The principal tasks of the men are the care of cattle and the building of houses. As regards the first, care and ownership are not necessarily coincident. Both women and men can own cattle, but more are owned by men than by women. It has not so far been found possible to form any exact notion of the proportion owned by the sexes. Also, more men own cattle than do women. A random sampling of 50 women and 40 men in one community showed that 46 per cent. of the women and 84 per cent. of the men are cattle-owners. Numerically, this would probably not be valid for a larger area; it does, however, give a limited statistical verification to a conclusion drawn from general observation. But, whoever the owner, the responsibility for the care of the cattle rests with the man; when a woman owns cattle, she gives her brother or her husband charge of them.

The care of cattle includes herding, milking, providing shelter, and, occasionally, treating for disease. The herding is done by young boys, 8 to 12 years of age, under the direction of their fathers. Lacking sons of a proper age, a man must either employ an older son, put the cattle in charge of a kinsman who has sons, or herd them himself. The milking is done by the man himself or by a son if he has one old enough. Treatment for disease only occurs in emergencies; there is no systematic preventive treatment.

The value of cattle, in terms of current real income, is small. Milk is welcome, both for cooking and for drinking; but it is not a food to be relied upon. Cows only yield milk when the calves are suckling, and even then in small quantities; the average yield does not exceed a pint and a half a day for each cow. Relative to the numbers owned, stock is seldom slaughtered for food or for the sale of meat. This use is forbidden by the slowness of the rate of increase. East coast fever claims a high percentage of the calves born every year.[1]

The Hehe value their cattle chiefly as currency and as a method of increasing their wealth, even though the rate of increase is small. As currency, cattle are used to make large traditional transfers of property;

---

[1] The disease is enzootic in the highland areas, and the mortality among the calves is believed to be as high as 50 per cent.

the bride-wealth is paid principally in cattle, and compensations are usually reckoned in cattle. The only use of cattle which brings no immediate profit is slaughtering for funerals or for prayers to ancestors. The first is necessary to social esteem, the second is believed to bring profit because it placates the ancestral spirits. As a means of increasing wealth, cattle do not deteriorate as does other property. One beast may die, but, at worst, as many are born as those which die; and, with luck, there will be more births than deaths. Cattle are thus used for ceremonial occasions and for ceremonial payments, but there is no trace of a ritual attitude towards cattle. They are valued for the ends, social or economic, which they accomplish, but only as a means to these ends. Moreover, they may be sold for money; the objections raised to selling are economic, not religious; and cattle play a limited, but unmistakable, part in the new money economics.

House-building is by no means a negligible task. The Hehe build generously and solidly. Whether their walls be of wattle and daub or of layered mud, they are no temporary shelters, but houses in which the family expect to live for many years. Their flat-arched roofs are an effective protection against rain, sun, and the extremes of temperature; and the accommodation, if primitive, is generous. Thus the task of building is no small part of the man's share of household labour.

For a man with one wife, three rooms are considered

necessary. There is first the *idama*, the entrance-room. In this the cattle are kept, the herd-boys sleep, and the cooking is done; or, if there are many cattle, there is a separate *idama* for cooking. Next comes the *bwalo*, the social centre of the house. Beer is served here when large parties assemble, the head of the house uses it for his household tasks, and the younger children sleep in it at night. Finally, the *gati* is the bedroom. This is specifically the woman's room. She keeps her treasures in it, and no one may enter it without her permission, except her husband. If there are two wives, each must have her own *gati* and preferably her own *idama*; and a large number of wives necessitates many bedrooms and *madama* for cooking. The sizes of the rooms vary, but each bedroom is usually at least 13 feet wide and 13 to 20 feet long. The *bwalo*, of the same width, is from 20 to 30 feet long or even longer, while the *idama* may be either a small cooking- and entrance-room, or a long chamber as big as the *bwalo*, according to the number of the cattle. The rooms may be laid out in a row, or the house may be L-shaped or T-shaped, or may enclose three or four sides of a quadrangle. The standards here given may not always be observed—a man with only one wife, few children, and no cattle may content himself with only two rooms; a man with many wives may never quite keep up with his building requirements—but the standard of accommodation is always there, and the majority of the tribe live up to the standard.

There are two types of houses,[1] the chief difference being in the walls. The old Hehe type consists of a wall of stout posts, firmly lashed together, over which mud is smeared inside and out—a particularly solid version of the wattle-and-daub style. The newer type is copied from the Bena,[2] and has a thick mud wall built up in layers, each layer being allowed to dry before the next is applied. In both cases the roof is the same: a shallow arch, resting on opposite walls, supported by two ridge-poles, overlaid by rafters, and reinforced by pillars. It is made waterproof by thatch into which mud is beaten.

Such a house demands a considerable amount of work. The rafters, beams, and pillars are numerous and take a long time to cut. A wattle-and-daub wall adds to the timber; a mud wall adds to the labour. House-building is usually begun after the rains. If a complete new house is built, it usually takes six to eight months; if a wing is being added, two to three months is generally necessary. Most men repair or add to their houses every year. A new house is built every ten or twelve years; and the house must be re-roofed every four or five years.

The man is responsible for most of the work. He cuts the timber, builds the walls, and thatches. If he has sons, they help him regularly. In addition, his

---

[1] The architecture of a portion of the eastern and south-eastern section of the tribe is different structurally, but the standards of housing are the same.

[2] See above, p. 27.

wife has specific duties. She must carry the water for building the mud walls and she must supply the short grass which is put on the apex of the roof. But certain tasks require community co-operation, and the building of a house is periodically hastened by beer parties, on the same principle as co-operation in agriculture is organized. The wife's duties are thus added to by the task of preparing beer periodically. If much timber has been cut, there is a party for carrying it in. Another party adds to the grass for the thatch. Still another supplies the reeds which, woven into a mat, go between rafter and thatch; and a final, indispensable party must be given for the placing of the mat and the final roofing. In these parties, the division of labour is still observed: women only perform women's tasks, men only men's. House-building thus involves co-operation between men of the community, as well as subsidiary, but necessary, assistance from women. As in agriculture, the bulk of the co-operative work is done by a small number of men whose obligations to the builder are binding; and there are the usual number of drones who drink but do not work.

Women's tasks, apart from agriculture, are most concerned with the routine of the household. They husk, pound, and grind the maize, cook the food, carry the water, and prepare the beer; and they are generally responsible for the maintenance of the house. These tasks demand more continuous effort than those of the men; a man may work hard for days or weeks, but he can always rest; if a woman ceases work, the household routine suffers.

The crafts of the Hehe are relatively few in number. They are subject to a strict sex-division of labour. The men's crafts are smithing and woodworking; the women's plaiting and pottery.

Of these crafts, the most distinctive is smithing. The smiths are a limited group and form the nearest approach to an organized craft to be found among the Hehe. A man usually acquires his knowledge from his father, from working with him for years; but a nephew or a son-in-law may also be taught. A stranger may be initiated into the secrets of the craft, but only on the payment of a specified number of cattle. Smiths form a group, not only because the acquisition of skill requires much practice, but because secret knowledge is also necessary. A smith must know the proper medicines; there are medicines for tempering, for welding, and for working iron. There is, moreover, a special smiths' medicine for summoning other smiths to one's assistance; the user of it vaccinates himself, utters a formula, and other smiths must come to his aid. We have not heard that this medicine has been used in recent years; but knowledge of it is still taught. Smiths, although forming a well-marked group, are not a caste separated from their fellows. They live the same social life and perform the same agricultural tasks as their neighbours; and they are on terms of equality with other members of the community. Their products offer little variety and consist of spears, bill-hooks, axes, hoes, bells, razors, and adzes.

Woodworking is practised by all the men of the tribe. Every man makes his own hoe-handles, his axe-hafts, his spear-shafts, and various other objects of daily use. There are, however, several objects beyond the ordinary man's ability. Among these are stools, mortars for pounding grain, drums, and ornamented staves; these are made by men of recognized skill. It thus comes about that there are craftsmen in wood just as there are craftsmen in iron. But their positions are different: while the smith belongs to a well-marked group, the skilled woodworker is merely a man who has developed a recognized superiority in a craft practised by all.

All women are generally expected to be able to plait their own baskets and to make their own pots, but not all do so. We have found that about 75 per cent. of the women know how to plait, but only about 30 per cent. can make pots; and among these there are gradations of skill. Plaited work includes baskets of various sizes and shapes for carrying or storing maize, flour, and other food-stuffs, and also flask-shaped drinking-cups. Pots are also of many sizes and shapes; for cooking and eating food, for cooking beer, and for storing water. Their capacity varies from a liquid quart to 16 gallons.

The iron, wooden, plaited, and earthen objects are not made by every one, yet they are required in every household. This necessitates some system of purchase. The traditional system is neither purchase with recognized currency nor barter, but is based on an exchange of services. If a spear is required, the purchaser first supplies iron, in excess of what is needed. He must then bring in charcoal, more than is required. During the time his spear is being made, he must either assist the smith at his task, or must cultivate the smith's plantations. If a stool is wanted, the purchaser cuts a piece of timber large enough to make two stools. If a pot is required, the purchaser supplies more clay than is needed and assists at the less skilled tasks of pottery. In each case, the principle is not the exchange of the products of two special skills, but the offer of unskilled labour for the required product. The profit of the artisan lies in having his unskilled tasks performed for him and in the accumulation of the raw materials of his craft. In the olden days, these raw materials were used to make artifacts for the chief or the sub-chief; and if the recipients were pleased, they responded with gifts of cattle. The system is now in the process of breaking down. Many men living the traditional life still satisfy their traditional needs in the old way, but many others purchase for money; and the craftsman's surplus materials nearly always go to making objects for sale. It is probable that in the next generation all products of special skill will be sold for money.

The money economy of the tribe has developed on account of two needs: to pay taxes and to buy imported goods. The first necessity was created, of course, by the Government. The year after the conquest of the tribe, a tax of maize was levied. Two years later a money-tax of 1 rupee for every able-bodied male was substituted. This was gradually raised to 3 rupees.[1] When the British took over the administration, a hut and poll-tax of 6 shillings was imposed. In 1925 this was raised to 10 shillings. In 1932 the plural wives' tax was first introduced; single men or men with one wife now pay 8 shillings; the tax for each additional wife is 2 shillings.

Although taxation was probably the first incentive to obtain money, the demand for imported goods followed close behind. Before their conquest, the Hehe had used cloth, distributed by the chief as explained above.[2] A limited demand grew up for other goods: powder for muskets, knives, umbrellas, and, more recently, soap. Cloth, however, continues to be the imported commodity in greatest demand.

We have found it impossible to trace, with any accuracy, the details of the growth of a money economy since 1898. In that year, money was unknown; now it has penetrated every aspect of native economic life.

Money is obtained by working for wages and by the sale of produce and of stock.[3] These items account

---

[1] The details of the tax levied by the German administration were given us by native informants. We have been unable to verify them by reference to official records.

[2] See above, p. 32.

[3] See Appendix C, answer to question No. 33, pp. 256–62, where such statistics as we have been able to compile are given in full.

for nearly all the annual cash income of an ordinary tribesman. Wages account for 32 per cent. of the total incomes; and about half the able-bodied men work for wages for one, two, or three months a year. Wages for unskilled labour vary from 6 to 10 shillings a month, and may average between 7 and 8 shillings.[1]

In seeking work, the Hehe prefer to remain as near home as possible, and very few go outside the Iringa District. Work is procurable on government works, on European plantations, and in the township, where traders employ a small number of labourers. The missions also employ a certain number of men for building and for the cultivation of their plantations. Some kinds of work are more popular than others, but the chief considerations are always the nearness to home and the character of the employer. The wage offered is a subsidiary, though not unimportant, consideration. Thus, at one time, work on the roads was avoided when other work was procurable, because the European in charge was unpopular and because it took the men far from home; and difficulty was experienced in obtaining sufficient labour, even though the wages offered were higher than those offered by private employers. Later, this work became more popular, because there was a different European in charge. Among the planters, some can get all the labour they wish, offering the minimum wage; others

[1] This estimate is for 1933. Wages were higher for previous years. We have not estimated the wages paid to women, as very few go out to work, either casually or permanently.

can never get enough, offering much higher wages. On the whole, the Hehe do not like working for wages. They must get the money, and many prefer work to parting with their stock, but work is accepted as a necessary evil. Consequently, they are careful in their selection of an employer.

Among employers, there is a great diversity of opinion as to the value of the Hehe as labourers. Some planters prefer not to have them at all and employ the neighbouring Bena and Kinga, who are more docile. Others are finding them satisfactory: these claim that the Hehe are hard to get on with at first, but that once they decide they are getting fair and reasonable treatment, they are more intelligent workmen than the men of other tribes. It is noteworthy that on the plantations of those employers who prefer them, there is a growing number of Hehe who work for long periods at a time, and some even form a permanent labour force.

Of the Hehe who do not rely upon wages as their chief source of cash income, the majority sell part of their crops or their cattle. The principal cash crop is maize. This is sold in the Iringa market, either in whole grain or as flour. It is also sold to the small native or Indian shops scattered throughout the tribe. The amount sold by each householder is not large. Most of them sell not more than a sack; very commonly only half a sack is sold in a year. Potatoes, milk, onions, eggs, and chickens are sold in small quantities. Cattle are always saleable; they are sometimes sold on the hoof, at other times slaughtered for the sale of the meat. An ox will fetch from 7 to 14 shillings, a cow from 15 to 20 shillings.

These and subsidiary sources of income procure for the Hehe, on the average, 30 shillings a year. Of this, 31 per cent. is paid out in taxes, 46 per cent. is spent on clothes, and the remainder on hoes,[1] soap, and other imported goods, or, within the tribe, on beer, native medicine, maize, and ceremonial payments.

The estimates given above are for Hehe living the tribal life, for whom the sale of produce only means a small increase in the area of land cultivated in the traditional manner, and for whom labour for wages is an incident in their lives, not a permanent means of subsistence, nor a mode of living. There are, however, a small number of Hehe who work regularly for wages and whose cash income is therefore higher. These are government and mission teachers, craftsmen, permanent government employees, those paid by the native administration, permanent employees on European plantations, and servants of Europeans and Indians. Many of these positions are occupied by men of other tribes; the exact number of Hehe so employed is not known; but we have made a rough estimate and have come to the conclusion that between 800 and 900 are in continual employment. Since the number of tax-payers in the tribe is about

---

[1] The excellent native-made hoe is being replaced by an imported article which is cheaper, but which does not last as long.

17,000,[1] the number permanently employed is about 5 per cent. of the men of the tribe.

From all these figures, we can form a general idea of the total annual income of the tribe. Assuming that the estimate of 30 shillings per annum for each tax-payer holds for the whole tribe,[2] the total income would be £25,500. In addition to this, we have estimated that the 800 or 900 natives in permanent employment make a total annual income of £6,000;[3] the total income is therefore £31,500.

This estimate, rough as it is, may give some idea of the amount of money in circulation in the tribe itself. Of the total income, probably 85 per cent. goes for payment of tax and for the purchase of imported goods. That leaves 15 per cent. or approximately £4,725 for intra-tribal transactions. Most of this money is spent in the purchase of food, cattle, beer, native artifacts, native medicine, and for ceremonial payments.

This amount, although small for a population of over 86,000, is yet sufficient to account for the growth of a money economy within the tribe itself. This money economy is still in a rudimentary stage, and

[1] The official figure is 17,423.

[2] It is possible that adequate statistics would not bear out this assumption. But it is also probable that the average annual income in any area would not be less than 20 shillings; in some small areas it is certainly more than 30 shillings; therefore 30 shillings may be an over-estimate, but will probably be correct to within 20 per cent.

[3] The average wage for permanent, semi-skilled or skilled labour thus works out at approximately 12 shillings per month.

many economic transactions are still conducted in the traditional manner; but it permeates, in some degree, all aspects of the Hehe economic life. In agriculture, for instance, there is now an accepted payment for the cultivation of the plantations: Hehe who are in permanent employment may have their plots cultivated at a charge of one shilling and fifty cents for each *mgunda*. Cattle frequently change hands, at market rates. Foodstuffs are sold at prevailing prices, which vary according to the time of the year. And more and more products of native craftsmanship are being sold for cash. At what is little more than a guess, it might be said that half the transactions between tribesmen are conducted on a money basis.

As marking the growth of a money economy, it is significant that most transactions are stated in terms of money, even if the payments are made in kind. Native medicines are often paid for in kind, but an exact equivalent in money is preferred; and some native doctors insist upon money. The bride-wealth is stated in terms of cattle, sheep, and hoes, together with a money payment, but a total money value is generally reckoned and accepted, if offered; it is, indeed, often preferred. Meat or beer sold is always priced in terms of money, but maize may be accepted instead. In brief, while there is not enough money in circulation within the tribe to conduct all transactions through its medium, yet the tendency is now to reckon all economic activities in money terms; and if the prosperity of the tribe increases sufficiently, it is probable that all exchange of goods and services will be for money, except, perhaps, the co-operative exchange of labour in the cultivation of the soil.

Any improvement in the economic status of the Hehe must be based upon the cultivation of larger areas of foodstuffs, upon the introduction of higher-priced economic crops, upon a more efficient utilization of the economic possibilities of their cattle, or upon the extension of their wage-earning capacities. Probably such improvement as takes place will result from the realization of all these possibilities.

First, more foodstuffs can be grown by the present methods of agriculture. Already, in the last two or three years, larger areas have been put under cultivation than previously; each household grows more maize, and the introduction of cassava does not mean the replacement of other crops, but adds to the food-supply. This increase is partly the result of a gradually expanding market, partly because of instructions issued by the administration. The area under cultivation could be still further extended, but the possible extension cannot go beyond a certain point. While the hoe is the only agricultural implement, the amount of land which can be cultivated is limited by the physical capacities of the household.[1] Moreover, the planting-season does not extend beyond six weeks or at most two months.

If we assume that the incentives were sufficient to

[1] The possibility of a larger yield per acre has not been considered here, as it is primarily a technical agricultural problem.

cause marked increase in agricultural production, it is important to consider its social as well as its economic effects. We believe that if cultivation were done to the maximum of physical capacity, the result would be a great readjustment in the relationship between the sexes. At present, women do more cultivation than men. If cultivation were increased, the men would have to do a larger proportion, because the time available to the women for work in the fields is restricted by other duties. The Hehe woman has a number of daily tasks which often keep her steadily busy from dawn to sunset, with a short break in the middle of the day. This routine is heavy, but it is subject to ameliorations. First, the tasks are varied, and difficult physical toil can be alternated with lighter household duties. Secondly, she has complete disposal of her own time: if she is lazy, her husband and family will lament it, but it will be accepted by the neighbourhood that 'she is like that', and she will suffer little social inconvenience. Thirdly, women do much of their work together; they assist each other in carrying water when beer is being prepared by one of them, they work together in the field, and they co-operate in the pounding of corn; heavy tasks are thus not only shared, but lightened by the pleasures of companionship. Fourthly, their many kinship obligations give women legitimate excuses to visit their relatives at intervals, thus giving them a complete rest from routine. Thus it is an exaggeration to say that they are overworked: while some of them find their duties too much for them, the large majority retain their health and spirits to an almost surprising degree. Nevertheless, their time is very fully occupied; and any considerable increase of work might easily overburden them.

The men, on the other hand, are not the servants of routine. Such tasks as house-building impose heavy work upon them for short intervals, but their time is much their own. Even during the planting, when a man undertakes a not inconsiderable share of the labour, he has more free time than his wife. Thus any marked increase in the production of foodstuffs would have to depend upon the labour of the men.

This would change the relationship between the sexes in two ways. First, it would increase the economic dominance of the men. It has been explained that crops grown by men are their personal property, while those of the women are jointly owned. The other change would be of less benefit to the men. Their present comparative freedom from routine work gives them the opportunity, which they so prize, of attending to community and tribal affairs, of reinforcing the bonds of kinship by visits to distant relatives, and of pursuing their individual interests. An increase in their agricultural work would make them more like peasants and less like men of public affairs. Neither of these changes would be necessarily disadvantageous to certain aspects of tribal life; but it would mean a notable alteration in the relationship between men and women and in the quality of native public life.

The possible increase in agricultural production might be as much as one-half of the present production, though this is little more than a guess. But it is improbable that the increase would be nearly so much. Maize, the principal product, is not of sufficient value to stand the transport charges to the railway, and the Hehe must rely upon a local market. This is restricted and could not absorb the potential increase in production. Since the uneaten and unsold maize could only rot, the production will probably not show a marked increase; even the present small increases will not continue if reasonable prices are not obtained.

The introduction of a high-priced crop is not easy. The northern part of the tribe, who live in a lower country, will be able to produce rice in increasing quantities; and other small sections can produce ground-nuts; but the crops upon which many other tribes rely do not grow well in the Hehe country. Consequently the selection of a suitable cash crop is difficult. Experiments are now being made with peas and heavy tobacco, but there is not yet sufficient information available to say whether they will be of much future significance.

The better economic use of cattle also presents many difficulties. First, the incidence of east coast fever takes a heavy toll of the calves, so that the rate of increase is very slow. Secondly, even if this handicap were overcome it is probable that the market for meat or for cattle on the hoof would soon be saturated. The possibilities of utilizing the milk-supplies are also restricted. The milk-production is low; and, while the market can absorb much more than is at present produced, the organization is lacking. The European community requires milk for household use and for the making of butter, but this only affects natives living within a limited distance from the farms. The Indians make an excellent ghee from milk purchased from the natives, and some Indian merchants have established buying-posts, equipped with cream-separators, at various places in the District. But many areas are still untouched; a more widespread and efficient organization for the buying of milk is needed; and even granting that, the total milk-supply of the tribe is not sufficient to constitute, by itself, a very great addition to the tribal income.

These possibilities might be different if there were a general improvement in the breeding and the care of the stock. There is at present no selection in breeding; the housing is bad; the cattle are not grazed sufficiently; calves do not get sufficient milk; and there is no attempt at providing fodder during the worst part of the dry season. An improvement in the general care of the cattle might mean less mortality from east coast fever and an improvement in their general condition. Thus, even if markets do not expand to any extent, such profits as are at present derived from the ownership of cattle might increase, because of improved quality; and there would be more chance of increase in the stock. This, in turn, would increase the supply of manure, which is essential to the production of economically valuable crops. A more thorough attention to cattle-raising would necessitate a social change. Most of the labour involved is now done by boys; they herd and milk, though the houses for cattle are made by the men. If animal husbandry were taken seriously, men would have to devote more time and attention to it. This, in turn, would probably involve other changes in the family and community distribution of tasks.

The final possibility, the increase in the amount of wage-labour, depends upon two factors: the success of the European plantations and the adaptation of the Hehe to labour conditions. The first we are not qualified to discuss. Regarding the second, we have already mentioned that the Hehe are not considered by many settlers as good labourers and that they are rather careful in their choice of employers. The result is that, of the labourers employed on the farms and plantations in the District, probably rather less than half are Hehe. If European plantations prosper, the Hehe may be induced to go out to work in increasing numbers. If anticipated developments do not take place, they will have to make themselves more adaptable to labour conditions than they are at present. Their willingness to do this depends upon the development of the other possibilities of economic betterment.

If the Hehe must rely primarily upon the development of a peasant economy, their principal efforts will have to be directed towards the production of high-priced crops, so that they can depend upon the export trade, or at least upon markets beyond their own District. If such a development is shown to be possible, it will be necessary to adapt the Hehe economic organization to the new economic situation which will arise. On the production side, there will be problems of seed-selection, of planting and caring for the crop, and of proper treatment after harvest. If the crop is a highly specialized one, the purchase of suitable implements and the building up of capital equipment may prove to be necessary. On the marketing side, problems of selection and grading will doubtless demand attention. These technical problems are beyond our scope; all we wish to do here is to indicate the possibility of their occurrence and to discuss the questions of social organization which they will entail.

If capital equipment and group marketing is necessary, the individual Hehe is too poor and too ignorant to meet the situation by himself, and some form of co-operative effort will be necessary. The particular form of co-operation will depend upon the nature of the crop and the markets; what we are concerned with is to indicate the existence of social groupings which may be adapted to the new circumstances. In our opinion, only one such grouping is in existence. The Hehe system of co-operation in agriculture depends upon kinship and neighbourhood. Kinship by itself is economically insufficient, because kindred are scattered over wide areas of country. Neighbourhood by itself is insufficient, because mutual obligations are not sufficiently binding. But in a settlement (*lilungulu*), neighbourhood and kinship generally go hand in hand. Even if totally unrelated families become members of the same settlement, intermarriage occurs and kinship bonds reinforce those of common membership in a community. It is those who are both neighbours and relatives who form the present co-operative group; and it is possible that this kinship-settlement group may be utilized for more complex undertakings. At present, co-operation is confined to a customary, limited exchange of labour in the cultivation of the soil and other traditional tasks. Any attempt to develop new forms of co-operation would involve the development of new social concepts and new group obligations. It is quite within the bounds of possibility that different groups will be more efficient: mission centres, for example, may create more effective units for co-operation in the preparation and marketing of economic crops than indigenous groups. All that can be said is that, in our opinion, if indigenous institutions are to be the social bases of co-operation, the kinship-settlement grouping is that which holds the most promise.

The Hehe political organization, we believe, can only be adapted for limited and simple economic ends. It might be used for the purchase of equipment and seed and for the buying up and disposal of crops which have a stable market; but its use even for these purposes would involve a considerable amount of supervision. It can reinforce traditional or accepted activities, but cannot institute new ones. Thus it has been suggested that each headman enforce the cultivation of a communal plantation as an insurance against famine. This would be feasible, if there were sufficient supervision and if penalties were exacted for non-compliance with instructions; but even with all these conditions, it is only possible if a standard crop, the cultivation of which is well understood, is adopted. The native authorities are effective in their sphere, but new responsibilities must be thrust upon them with great caution; and we believe that new agricultural methods can be developed best by other agencies, such as those we have suggested.

E. *RELIGION*

The religion of the Hehe may, superficially, be called ancestor-worship, for its basis is a system of ceremonial sacrifice and supplication to the souls of dead ancestors. But to call it 'worship', in the European sense of the term, is to miss its significance. It is really a system of begging ancestral assistance in certain emergencies and of placating ancestral wrath which follows certain offences.

The essence of Hehe religion is not belief, but ritual. The European inquiring into the matter is apt to ask: What are the ancestral spirits (*misoka*)? Where do they live? How do they affect the life and well-being of their descendants? The answers given to these questions are unsatisfactory in the extreme. The *misoka* are the souls of those who have died, and are like air (*ng'ala*); they live at their graves and at cross-roads and everywhere and nowhere; and, in certain circumstances, they are a source of danger to the family; in others, their aid must be sought. The proper questions to ask the Hehe are: What help can ancestral spirits give their descendants? How can their aid be obtained? When are the ancestral spirits angry with their descendants? How can their anger be appeased? Hehe religion is a matter of ritual observances rather than belief.

The ancestral spirits must be supplicated when certain contingencies arise. Nowadays, one of the most important of such ceremonies is that of naming a child. At some period of a child's life, he cries excessively. From the European point of view, this may be due to malnutrition, teething, or some specific illness; the Hehe say he is crying for his name, for the name of some ancestor. A magician (*mlagusi*) is consulted; he resorts to divination and discovers that the child is crying for the name of a paternal or a maternal ancestor. The father of the child then arranges a rite, dedicated to the ancestor indicated. A sacrifice of flour and beer at the appropriate grave is prepared; this is put upon the grave in the evening; in the morning, when the sacrifice is accepted (that is, eaten by insects or animals), a simple prayer is offered. The ancestor is invoked by name; the contingency is stated; and the ancestor is asked to help the child throughout his life and to use his influence with other dead ancestors to help him in all contingencies. From one point of view, it is an attempt to secure extra-human assistance for the new member of the social group; from another point of view, it is a ritual inclusion of the child within the circle of kinship, which includes the dead as well as the living. Ancestral assistance is also invoked for dangerous journeys, for inexplicable illness, and to give rain. In every case it is the invocation of an ancestral spirit, belonging to the group of dead kindred, for assistance in emergency.

Besides these emergencies, ancestral kindred demand placation when certain offences have been committed. A father curses a son; the ancestral spirits are angry; the son cannot eat in the household without risk of illness and death; he must eat with people not kindred until the ancestral curse is ritually removed. Similarly, there may be a quarrel between close kindred; a childbirth may become overdue; it cannot take place until the ancestral dissatisfaction is removed. The quarrel is made up and the birth proceeds satisfactorily. In terms of belief, the ancestors abhor discord in the family; when it occurs, they become angry; a curse or penalty (*mmepo*) is put upon the persons concerned; and it can only be removed or averted by the observance of a suitable rite.

The Hehe religion is thus purely a family affair. Ancestral spirits concern themselves only with the affairs of their descendants. They are particularly concerned when violent family differences occur. And the ritual necessary to placate or to invoke them can only be performed by one of their descendants. Though dead, they still belong to the family. Though powerful, their ability to cause damage is confined to their living kindred. In death, they are still members of the circle of effective kinship.

The rites attendant upon communion with ancestors are simple in the extreme. The essential element is the sacrifice (*nambiko*). In relatively unimportant matters, flour and unfermented beer are offered; in more serious cases, a sheep is slaughtered; in the most important cases, an ox is the sacrifice. But the term 'sacrifice' may give a false impression. The offerings are not a gift to the ancestral spirits, offered as a bribe. What is offered to the ancestors must be partaken by those making the offering. Thus, if flour is offered, those conducting the ceremony must also eat a little of it; if unfermented beer is offered, all kinsmen concerned must be sprinkled with it; and if a sheep or an ox is offered, the ancestors are given the lungs and the meat from the shoulder-blade; the rest of the animal is distributed to the assembled kinsmen and cooked and eaten. The fundamental necessity is a communion of food, not a gift in return for services.

The relationship between ancestral spirits and the living family is not confined to intervention on special occasions. One of the more important functions of the *misoka* is to assist in the practice of medicine. There are two kinds of native practitioners: the *mlagusi*, or diviner, and the *mukofi*, or digger of medicine. Usually the diviner is also a digger. Knowledge of the digging and preparation of medicine is derived, directly or remotely, from ancestral spirits. A dispenser of medicines may have learnt from his own ancestral spirits, he may have been taught by a father, the genealogy of the medicine may go through several generations, but it is always traceable to some one who learnt it from the *misoka*.

Diviners are of two kinds: there are those who use instruments of divination, the commonest of which are the divining-sticks (*ngelo*); and there are those who put themselves into direct communication with their ancestors for every act of divination. We have listed sixty-four diviners; of these, twenty-nine deal directly with their *misoka*. Direct communications from ancestral spirits may be received by the *mlagusi* when he is asleep; or they may be received when he is in a condition of voluntary or involuntary dissociation. The methods of invoking ancestral aid vary: some diviners perform certain rites, some utter a formula, and some swallow medicines. The chief point to be made here is that they are in continual communication with their ancestors, who thus exert a profound influence upon their lives.

We have already described how this familial religion can become tribal; the family and the ancestors of the ruling chief are associated with tribal well-being. Thus the chief can invoke his ancestors for assistance for the whole tribe; the sub-chief or headman can do likewise for the territory he governs. Nowadays, the tribal prayers are principally for rain;

in the olden days, aid in war was invoked. The ancestors of the chiefs do not thus become tribal gods; they remain ancestors of one family, but ancestors whose special position gives them wide powers.

In addition to ancestral spirits, the Hehe believe in a god, *nguluvi*. This god is believed in, but not worshipped. He is remote from the affairs of men and only concerns himself with general events, not with the fate of individuals. Generally, his name is used to explain phenomena beyond the comprehension or interest of the tribe. When a child dies, they say '*ahele kunguluvi*', 'he has gone to god'; that is, they do not know what becomes of him. (A dead child does not become an ancestral spirit.) When asked what causes locusts, one is told '*nguluvi hela*', 'god only', meaning that they do not know. *Nguluvi* has no definite attributes; and he demands and receives no ritual recognition. *Nguluvi* is little more than a word, and does not constitute an effective part of Hehe religion.

It is probable that the Hehe religion is doomed as a system of beliefs or of ceremonies. The Hehe have, in the first generation of foreign contact, shown a passive resistance to the new creeds. Mohammedanism first appeared in the tribe a few years after their conquest, and Mohammedans now number about 9,000.[1] The Tosamaganga Mission was founded in

---

[1] Of these, a good many are members of other tribes, who live in the District. We have not been able to make any estimate of the number of actual Hehe who are Mohammedans, but believe that a majority of the 9,000 are Hehe converts.

1896, by the German Benedictines. The fathers of the Italian Consolata Mission, who took over Tosamaganga from the Benedictines in 1923, claim that they have 3,000 converts and a further 11,000 adherents. The proselytes of the Berlin Lutheran Mission, which only re-established a station in the Iringa District in 1931, after a lapse of seventeen years, but which has had some influence on those living near the Bena border since early in the century, are few in number. This leaves a majority of the tribe pagan, and Christianity is not yet the dominant religious factor. Christians do not boast of their religion. While a Christian would be unlikely to deny his faith, yet he does not generally mention it, unless he is asked. And Christianity has one very serious drawback in Hehe eyes: it does not permit polygyny. But mission activity is increasing in intensity and in extent; and we believe that in another twenty years a very large majority of the tribe will be Christian or Mohammedan, with the Christians predominating.

The effect of the new religious beliefs will be discussed in the next chapter.

F. OTHER CUSTOMS

This section deals with certain customs about which questions were asked, but to which the answers were to be limited in scope. They have been put together here because of the brief manner in which they were treated. In a more comprehensive work, of course, each subject of this section would either be dealt with at much greater length, or would belong to a larger field of culture not here treated fully.

1. STORIES AND TRADITIONAL HISTORIES

We have already noted that myths do not exist in this tribe, and that the stories which are told most often are the traditional histories of the ruling family and of former ruling families. We have indicated their sociological importance and their relationship to the tribal organization.[1] It only remains to make one comment on them. They are, as public tribal knowledge, in a constant process of contraction. This contraction shows itself in two ways. There is, first, a genealogical contraction. The Muyinga family count the present chief, Sapi, as the ninth descendant of the original founder of the family. In popular belief, he is the fourth or fifth. Secondly, events which older tradition[2] associates with the grandfather or great grandfather of the present chief are now associated with his father, Mkwawa. This process of contraction is probably related to the severely practical attitude the tribe adopts regarding traditional history—it is the tradition which matters, not the history. It is thus important to know that the present chief holds his power by hereditary right, but it does not matter to a generation or so how far back the right goes. Consequently, in collecting details of traditional history, many versions are given; the events are the same or similar, but the

[1] See above, pp. 24 and 39.
[2] Cf. Nigmann, E., *Die Wahehe*, Mittler und Sohn, Berlin, 1908.

persons who appear in them are different. The process of contraction does not hold universally. Close relatives of the chief can still give the full genealogy of the family (assuming that this has not previously been contracted); other families, formerly eminent, have even longer genealogies, the Nyentsa family, for example, tracing descent for fifteen generations. But this fuller knowledge is usually confined to relatively few members of each family, and the majority of people are satisfied with the shorter versions.

There are a few legends in the tribal lore. These are mostly told of older chiefs, or well-known magicians or warriors. They are only indirectly of sociological importance. They do not pretend to give the origins of customs, but the customary social values are assumed to have existed prior to the time of the legends. The Hehe legends have no social or moral purpose; they are merely stories of people who have lived in the past, or else stories of the past which have become attached to certain traditional figures.

There are stories of another kind called *nsimo* (sing. *lusimo*). These are folk-tales, told merely for amusement. Sociologically, they are only interesting because they illustrate social standards; like the legends, they do not explain or justify them. Thus in one such tale two girls marry two strangers against the wishes of their parents, and, as a consequence, narrowly escape being eaten by their new husbands. Girls should follow their parents' wishes and should choose as husbands men known to the community. The story is not told to point the moral; the moral is assumed before the story is told. Other stories are animal-tales; but, while vigorous enough, they lack the variety and ingenuity found in the tales of many African tribes.

Considered generally, the narratives of the Hehe are scanty and unimportant; and, sociologically, the most significant are those giving the traditional history of the formation of the tribe.

2. MAGIC AND WITCHCRAFT

Magic and witchcraft are not so sharply distinct among the Hehe as is the case in certain other tribes. The methods of the one are similar to the methods of the other, and the principal differences are the purposes of each and the social attitudes towards them. We shall, therefore, first show how both magic and witchcraft fit into one continuous system, and then indicate those factors which differentiate them.

Magic always involves the use of medicine, and it might have been preferable to use the latter term. The practice of magic or of medicine has two aspects. First, it is a method of finding out certain facts by divination (*kulagula*). Secondly, it is a means of accomplishing certain specific ends by the use of medicine (*mugoda*). Corresponding to these two aspects, there are two kinds of practitioner: the diviner (*mlagusi*), who controls the methods of discovering the required facts; and the maker of medicines. The latter is called a *mukofi*, literally a digger, since nearly all Hehe medicines are made from roots, although a few are made of twigs, leaves, and grasses. The diviner is always a digger of medicine as well; hence the essential distinction is between a practitioner who also divines, and a simple practitioner. We have already indicated that all knowledge of medicine and all power of divination come, directly or indirectly, from the ancestral spirits.

Divination is practised by a variety of means; but the two most common are direct communication with the ancestral spirits and the divining-sticks (*ngelo*). The ordinary procedure is as follows. The individual seeking assistance comes to the diviner and merely states that something is the matter (*ndina lukani*, literally 'I have news'). The diviner must then state the nature of the trouble. If he states his patient's trouble correctly—the nature of the illness, family troubles, or lack of children—he is then asked to state the cause. He again resorts to divination and informs the patient of the reason for the illness: anger of the ancestral spirits, witchcraft, medicine used against him, or whatever it may be. He also informs the patient that he must procure medicine from a digger. The patient usually invites him to supply the medicine himself. A fee is paid for the divination, but the medicine is not paid for until the patient is cured.

A simple practitioner is usually applied to for a simple medicine for a recognized illness, or for some purpose not requiring divination, such as medicine for ensuring fertility of a garden. In these cases also, no fee is paid until the medicine has proved itself.

For the Hehe, medicine is a substance which, if properly administered or applied, will accomplish certain results. The basis of magical practice is the medicine itself. No magical rite is considered efficacious if there is no medicine; and, for the accomplishment of most purposes, the use of the proper medicine is sufficient. But sometimes certain rites are also necessary. Thus one cure for snake-bite must be bitten into the wound by the practitioner; medicines for some illnesses must be handed to the patient in specific ways; and medicines of purification, when the ancestral ghosts are angry, involve a complex system of rites. Similarly the use of a few medicines demands a special condition of the performer to make them efficacious. One magician has a medicine giving invulnerability to gun or rifle bullets. To administer it properly, he must refrain from sexual intercourse the night before and must perform all his rites and administer the medicine without speaking. But the medicine itself is the important factor; rite and condition of the performer are secondary.

Medicine is used for purposes which may be classified into three groups. First, there are medicines for purposes which are socially approved. These would include the medicines for the cure of illness, fertility medicines, medicines to increase the yield of maize, medicines for averting specific dangers, and ritual medicines, such as those given at a girl's initiation. Secondly, there are medicines to which society is morally indifferent; these are chiefly medicines for the promotion of purely individual ends. This group includes medicines for procuring wives; medicines a man administers to a wife to cause death to any one committing adultery with her (*lutambulilo*); medicines for catching or killing a thief (*kutega mutego*); and love philtres. Finally, there are medicines for purposes which are socially condemned. These are used to cause loss, injury, or death to an enemy. A person who employs medicines of this sort practises witchcraft (*uhavi*) and is called a witch or warlock (*muhavi*).

The belief in witchcraft has a different psychological basis from the belief in magic. Magic, as we have suggested, is an attempt to control the environment by the proper use of medicine; witchcraft is a means of explaining death or misfortune. Death and serious misfortune are not believed to occur from natural causes; human agency is nearly always blamed. Thus a man may die because he has had intercourse with a woman who has been given medicine to kill adulterers; or he may have stolen something and been trapped by medicine for the prevention of theft. In such cases his family can take no action; his death is the result of medicine, but his own illegal act caused the medicine to operate. But more often his death is ascribed to the malicious use of bad medicine (*mugoda mwanangifu*) by an enemy. In this case the user of the medicine is condemned by the community and is a warlock; and the kinsmen of the dead man can take retaliatory measures. Besides deaths from human agency, there are relatively few cases for which other causes are given: some of these are the result of a *mmepo*, a penalty for the commission of a forbidden act; others come from *nguluvi*, when it is admitted that no cause can be discovered.

If death or illness from witchcraft is suspected, the fact may be determined by divination. Not all diviners will give witchcraft as a cause; others will state it as a cause, but will not name the guilty person; but there are a good many who will name the warlock. Nowadays belief in witchcraft has no satisfactory outlet; an accusation cannot be accepted in the native courts.[1] Sometimes the aggrieved parties resort to counter-magic, but in most cases there is nothing to do; and there remain suppressed hates, which occasionally break out into accusations and quarrels. We have already noted that, in the olden days, accusations of witchcraft were decided by the poison ordeal under the direction of the chief. The present situation as regards witchcraft is probably one of the least satisfactory results of European administration, from the native point of view. Belief in witchcraft survives almost intact, and there is no recognized method of dealing with it.

While all witchcraft relies upon the use of medicine, yet there is a distinction between medicines which are administered directly and those which act at a distance; and, while all men who use medicine to kill are warlocks, we believe that the man who has medicines

[1] The Native Courts have no jurisdiction to deal with cases of witchcraft.

which operate at a distance is more of a warlock and is regarded with more hate and more dread. The reasons for this distinction are probably two. Granted a belief in the efficacy of medicine, it is an easy extension to accept that some medicines, administered directly, will cause death or illness; but the man whose medicines work at a distance has powers one degree removed from the ordinary practitioner. The other reason lies in the nature of the menace. One can always protect oneself against medicine which must be injected or swallowed; there is no protection, except counter-magic, against medicines which never come near one.

Among the Hehe, witchcraft is important as a belief, as an explanation of death and misfortune, rather than as a demonstrable fact. The vast majority of accusations of witchcraft have no basis in fact: they are emotional outbursts, a protest against loss. But at the same time there are people who consciously practise witchcraft. We have had reports of complete confessions of witchcraft from people who hoped to save themselves from dying of small-pox,[1] and these have been amplified by reports of confessions due to remorse. The confessions were either of killings to increase one's power (killing a kinsman, for example, adds to the efficacy of other medicines); or they were of the ownership of medicine which would control

[1] The Hehe believe that if a man has small-pox he is usually a warlock and can recover only by confession. An innocent person may catch the disease, but will always recover.

the actions of lions and make them kill other people. One must discount confessions made in fear of death, and allowances must be made for the utterances of the mentally unbalanced; yet it seems probable that there are people who possess medicines which they believe will accomplish evil ends and who even believe that they have operated to kill. It is impossible to estimate how many real practitioners of witchcraft there are, but they are probably very few.

We do not believe that the actual physical damage caused by practising warlocks is very great. It is possible that some few die of fear, but we have not witnessed any deaths which could be attributed to that cause. The actual medicines we believe to be harmless; their effect is magical, and we do not think that there are any poisons indigenous to the tribe.[1] But there is one danger arising from the belief in witchcraft. If European poison falls into the hands of the Hehe, its use fits so well into their concepts that it may cause much mischief. This is not a hypothetical danger. In 1932 white arsenic began to circulate in the tribe. In the Wasa area alone, it is probable that at least six people were poisoned during a series of feuds; and possibly four more deaths were attributable to this cause.[2] The poison spread to many parts of the tribe; several headmen and at least two of the sub-

---

[1] This opinion cannot be proved, but it is supported by that of the Medical Officer of the District, Dr. W. Hood-Dye.

[2] Police investigation, however, failed to obtain sufficient evidence to prosecute.

chiefs are in possession of it. In 1933 the number of deaths seems to have diminished; but if the poison is still in the possession of the people who had it formerly, it is well within the bounds of possibility that a new series of poisonings may occur, as the result of new feuds. This, of course, is a by-product of witchcraft; but it is one which follows so naturally from Hehe belief that it may become the source of much danger in the future.

Witchcraft has been classified as a socially condemned practice. This is not quite the same as calling it anti-social, that is, a source of danger to society. The essence of witchcraft is the belief in it; and to judge it in terms of its value to society we must estimate the effects of the belief. First, it tends to accentuate the conservatism of the Hehe. No man must be too much in advance of his neighbours, or there is a danger that a jealous warlock will kill him by witchcraft. Thus a man must not wear clothes which differ too markedly from those of his neighbours, nor must he seek methods of gaining wealth or social superiority which involve too great a departure from the traditional tribal life. This conservatism, based on fear, is in conflict with the Hehe urge to seek social superiority. Many men insistently strive for superiority by the accumulation of wealth, by knowledge of medicine, and by accepting office in the tribal organization. In doing so they must risk jealousy, and either disregard the dangers of witchcraft or take measures against it by procuring protective magic. Witchcraft is thus both a conservative influence (but only one among many) and a factor which is in conflict with other social forces.

Fear of witchcraft also tends to reinforce obedience to the tribal authorities. A large proportion of the Hehe headmen and sub-chiefs accumulate medicines to strengthen their power, and many of these medicines are for causing loss or death to others. These rulers are consequently feared by their subjects; yet at the same time they do not incur the social condemnation which falls to a commoner if he is suspected of witchcraft. This use of witchcraft, however, works both ways. A man in authority practises it to strengthen his power, but a rival may collect medicine to overthrow him. We have seen this attempted in two localities. In each case a powerful and wealthy commoner thought, for various reasons, that he should be headman in place of the present occupant, and at great expense bought the services or the medicines of warlocks to kill or to render powerless his successful rival. Witchcraft can thus be a threat to authority, as well as its support.

The fact that witchcraft performs certain useful social functions does not mean that we try to defend it; we simply attempt to explain it as it is. It will probably tend to lose its power, but slowly; and, for several generations at least, it will continue to be a force to be reckoned with. Since it is a matter of belief rather than of actual demonstrable results, very little can be done against it directly; the gradual substitution of other concepts of causality is the only course to pursue. And the long continuance of belief in witchcraft in more civilized countries, with occasional survivals even to-day, does not suggest that this course will be either easy or rapid.

3. FEMALE INITIATION[1]

The girl's initiation rites take place when the parents judge that she is about to reach puberty. They must be accomplished before the first menstruation occurs; in Hehe belief, the rites are necessary to ensure fertility; and, if menstruation occurs before initiation, special medicines must be bought, at very great cost, to make good the neglect. There are no initiation schools; each girl is usually initiated by herself; but there may occasionally be two or three initiated together—half-sisters, classificatory sisters, or cousins.

There are three stages to the initiation ceremonies, of which the first is probably the most important. When, in the parents' opinion, the girl is approaching puberty, arrangements are made with old women, who are real or classificatory grandmothers, to perform all the necessary rites; mothers, and members of the mother's generation, are not permitted to be present. Usually there are two or three old women, one of them, recognized for her skill in such matters, taking the leading part. The evening before, offerings are made to the ancestral spirits. In the morning, sup-

[1] There is no male initiation in the tribe.

plications are made for help in performing the rites and special prayers are offered that all may go well. The initiation party then leaves the house and proceeds to a river. The party consists of the old women, the girl who is to be initiated, and one or more slightly older girls, who have already been initiated; they are called *vafudasi* and might be considered sponsors. A number of young married women usually accompany them.

At the river, or before it is reached, the girl and her sponsors are ordered to strip. Arrived at the riverside, the girl is ordered to lie down. She is supported by her *mufudasi* and her head and the upper part of her body are covered with a piece of cloth. The officiating grandmother then excises the hymen with an ordinary knife. Medicines are immediately applied to the wound; and after an interval the girl is ordered to sit up.

The next, and one of the most significant parts of the rites, is the singing of the *misimu*. These are instructional songs which have a very specific social purpose: they instruct the initiate, in clear and unmistakable terms, in the sexual and social duties connected with marriage. The songs themselves are obscure and symbolical; but each song is followed by a verbal explanation, which leaves no doubt as to its meaning.

The songs, which are also sung at marriage, are numerous; we possess texts of about 150. Only a selection of them are sung at the initiation rites, but, since the initiate learns them in the period which follows, we give a summary of their content. First, they teach the details of sexual union; and nothing is left to the imagination. Secondly, they inculcate the observances and avoidances associated with menstruation, pregnancy, and marriage. And finally, they instruct the initiate in her social duties before and after marriage—her duties to her husband, to her co-wives, to her parents, and to her husband's parents. The singing and explaining of these songs may entail a certain amount of verbal licence, but their purpose is instructional, not to say moral.

When a number of the *misimu* have been sung, the mother joins the party. She is shown the excised hymen, which is then thrown under a fruit-bearing tree so that the girl may be productive, as the tree is. Next, the girl bathes in the river. The party then returns to the house, singing songs of rejoicing. Native beer is served to all comers and the remainder of the ceremony is social. The old woman who conducts the whole ritual is given a present, usually an ox, by the girl's father. The girl herself is given a new cloth.

The rites are sometimes carried on into the second day. The girl must strip again, more *misimu* are sung, and a sharp blow is administered with a stick. But in many cases all the ritual of the first stage is completed on the first day. The whole rite is called *luwungu lwa kwivindi*, or *luwungu lwa kutambika kwivindi*.

Of the two other stages of the initiation rites, one is to celebrate the first menstruation and the second is the community celebration of the girl's new status. It is a matter of chance which comes first. The rites of the first menstruation are relatively simple. They occur at the cessation of the menstrual flow. A small amount of beer is prepared, the place where the girl slept during her period is ritually swept, the *misimu* are again sung, and the girl again bathes in the river. Only a few close relatives attend.

The community celebration, which usually occurs about a year after the first rites, is the occasion of a large gathering. Great quantities of beer are prepared and every one is invited to attend. In the morning the initiate goes to the river with a number of women (about twice as many as went for the first rites), strips, and again listens to the *misimu*. Many more of them are sung than during the previous rites; and they are better understood by the initiate, who has been taught them with some thoroughness in the interval since her first introduction to them. When the singing is over, she is chased into the river by her *mufudasi*; the other women walk into the river to greet her and to give her presents. Emerging from the river, the initiate puts on new clothes and the women return together to the house. A large number of guests are assembled. Many of them bring gifts of cloth or of money to the initiate. The remainder of the day and night is passed in drinking, singing, and dancing. This last stage of the rites is called the *luwungu lwa kuhalula*.

The Hehe believe that these rites are necessary to the fertility of the girl. They also consider that they are an introduction to adult status. Throughout the whole of the first ceremony, the girl is constantly told *veve muvina lino*, 'you are grown up now', and is admonished to behave accordingly. Sociologically, the second is the significant belief. Up to the time of initiation, the girl is considered immature and is supposed to have no thought of men; after the rites, she is treated as an adult and is immediately sought in marriage, though she does not necessarily marry for some time. The first rites speak for themselves in this respect. The attention of the initiate is most painfully drawn to her sexual functions; and the instruction she receives all points to the role she must play as a married woman. It is, in brief, a social translation from childhood to womanhood. The succeeding rites emphasize the point. The celebration of the first menstruation ritually marks her further progress to womanhood; and the *luvungu lwa kuhalula* is the reception by the community of a new adult.

Psychologically, the rites have probably a profound effect. The moral instruction is given a strong emotional background by the infliction of pain and by the dramatic presentation of new knowledge; and, during the succession of rites, the social and moral instruction is repeated under some variety of circumstance. It is probably an important determinant in the sex morality of the Hehe girl. Unlike some of the surrounding tribes, the Hehe unmarried woman is not promiscuous; the men pay tribute to her virtue when they confide that young girls are hard to seduce. This sexual morality is lost after marriage; a large majority of Hehe women commit adultery. But the other lessons are not lost; the wife may be sexually unfaithful to her husband, but she is careful to observe her other social and marital obligations; and, while it would not be true to say that this is all due to the initiation rites, yet they certainly play their part in imparting the social code to the individual.

III

THE CHANGING TRIBE

In the previous chapter we attempted to outline the culture of the tribe as it exists to-day. To do this, we dealt with many changes which have occurred in the last generation. In this chapter it is our intention to study some of the more important factors causing cultural change in the present generation.

Hehe culture is not static, but is in a continual process of change. This process did not begin with the European conquest of the tribe. We have already indicated that in the half-century preceding European occupation two very important developments took place. A strong centralized government was created, binding together a number of petty chieftainates; and an international trade was developed through the medium of Arab and Swahili[1] traders, resulting, among other things, in the almost universal use of cloth within the tribe. It is nevertheless true that the process of change has been immensely accelerated by more immediate contact with European culture, and there are signs that the rate of change is increasing progressively.

It is obviously a matter of the greatest importance for the administrator to understand the nature and extent of the developments which are taking place. If administration means anything, it means the

[1] Natives from the coast. From the Arabic *Sahil*, coast.

guiding of a people in such a manner that their social and economic evolution will ultimately prove beneficial. The process of change should allow of adaptation to new conditions, without, at the same time, destroying all that is healthy in the original social structure. Consequently we consider that the study of cultural change is not only essential to an applied anthropology but is the most important part of it.

We realize with regret that, in this respect, we have fallen short of our aims to a far greater extent than in any other part of our experiment. We have, it is hoped, touched sufficiently on the subject to indicate its significance, but we have by no means given it the thorough analysis it requires. This is partly due to the shortness of the time at our disposal. We had only approached the general question of social change, when the experiment had perforce to be brought to an end.[1] Nevertheless we offer our limited results in this field on account of the importance which we ascribe to such studies, and in the hope that they may contain useful suggestions for future research along these lines. The field is indeed a vast one; and it is only by the wise application of the knowledge gained from comprehensive research in it that the tutelage of the peoples who are not yet able to stand by themselves under the strenuous conditions of the modern world can best be undertaken.

[1] Due to the anthropologist having to leave the Territory to take up an appointment in Samoa.

A. ADMINISTRATION[1]

Up to the present, administration has been the most important influence on tribal life. It is chiefly due to administrative activities that the Hehe enjoy such benefits of civilized rule as have come their way—peace, settled government, and an effective legal system; and it is partly due to European administration that other benefits such as medical and educational services have reached a certain proportion of the tribe. This preponderance of the influence of administration may not last. Mission influence is spreading year by year and presents great latent possibilities; and European settlement has not yet developed sufficiently for its effects on the tribe to be properly gauged. Administration remains the dominant factor, therefore, but for how long we cannot say.

Administrative duties, in the narrower sense of the term, include supervision and direction of the tribal administration, of the native courts, and of tax assessment[2] and collection. In this section we propose to suggest a few of the problems which arise in connexion with the tribal political organization and the development of the native courts. Taxation will be discussed in the following section.

We have already stated that the tribal authorities give their people security of person and property and

---

[1] It is suggested that the reader glance at questions 44 to 56 inclusive, in Appendix C, pp. 252–3.

[2] The District Officer, of course, does not decide the amount of tax, but it is his duty to advise on it.

sufficient freedom from oppression to pursue their own economic and social development,[1] and that, on the whole, the tribe are loyal to their native rulers. We have also indicated that certain abuses still exist: a small amount of forced labour, unfair incidence of certain public obligations, petty corruption on the part of the headmen.[2] A further unfortunate element in the present tribal structure is the tendency of the chief to disregard the security of office of the headmen and to substitute his own kinsmen whenever he can. These abuses are all comparatively small; but they are based on certain defects in the constitution of the Hehe tribe, which may be the cause of future difficulties.

The fundamental lack is that there are insufficient internal checks to the authority of the tribal rulers. In the olden days the check was provided by political realities: appalling cruelties might be inflicted upon individuals, but large groups must not be antagonized or there was danger to the chieftainate. Nowadays, with the authority of the Government supporting that of the chief, the political reality is different. There is no perceptible danger of tribal opinion expressing itself by revolution or secession, so the chief and each sub-chief and headman may proceed to seize such authority as is possible. The principal check is from above, not below. The chief, while he exercises such powers and enjoys such perquisites as he can, is

---

[1] See above, Chapter II, section A 1 (e), pp. 79–82.
[2] See above, Chapter II, section A 1 (d), pp. 64–5.

careful to avoid any acts which will involve him in trouble with the Government. Similarly the subordinate authorities try to avoid getting into trouble with the chief. There is an ultimate check from below: if matters became too bad, the people would probably either develop some form of passive resistance, or would make an appeal to the higher authorities. But within the limits thus imposed there is a considerable latitude for the tribal rulers to experiment as to the extent of their powers. The fundamental defect is that there is no adequate expression of public opinion upon administrative affairs, and thus no internal constitutional check upon the tribal authorities.

As education spreads, the expression of some sort of public opinion will develop; but this may bring dangers of its own. If the tribal constitution proves incapable of organizing and giving effect to growing public opinion, rulers and ruled will become estranged, and, as education spreads among the bulk of the tribe, the hostility to the native authorities may cause a break-down in the whole system of government. We suggest, therefore, that the vital functions of the administrator are, first, the maintenance of an adequate control over the tribal institutions, so that abuses are checked and causes for dissatisfaction removed; and secondly, the continuous evolution of the tribal institutions, so that effective expression can be given to the wishes of the tribe upon matters of internal policy.

We have no suggestions as to how this latter aim

could be realized; we believe that constitutional development must occur as need dictates and as circumstances arise. It is possible that the essential democracy at present apparent in the native courts might be adapted to the political sphere; or the annual gathering[1] might be utilized to secure a systematic and organized method of registering, and when possible acting upon, tribal opinion. At present no suitable institution exists.

The evolution of an effective tribal constitution will involve innumerable points of detail, of which we only suggest one. The scale of tribal salaries is at present badly drawn up. The higher authorities are paid in proper proportion, but the headman, upon whom the effective administration ultimately rests, is paid less than a tribal clerk; and many are paid even less than the tribal messengers. If educated Hehe are to be prevailed upon to accept these posts, and if the headmen are to be induced or forced to give up their present illegal perquisites, then their salaries will have to be adjusted in relation to their position. If this is not done, the educated and able men will not have sufficient inducement to accept the position of headmen. The tribal authorities will consequently lose the respect of the educated tribesmen, to the detriment of constitutional development.

While not directly connected with the evolution of

[1] Held at the chief's head-quarters once a year and presided over by the District Officer. At this gathering, matters pertaining to the administration of the tribe are discussed by all those present.

effective government to meet changing circumstances, the problem of the administration of the Iringa township is one which requires consideration. It has a native population of about 2,500, and, unlike other towns in the Territory, it is incorporated into the tribe and is governed by a sub-chief, who exercises his authority under the chief. The system works well, but largely on account of the abilities of the sub-chief; and we think both town and tribe would profit if they were separated. The town has problems of its own. It is composed of members of many tribes, and its social organization is consequently different from that of the country-dwelling Hehe and in a process of quicker change. The administration of justice is very complex. Hehe customs must sometimes be the decisive factor, Mohammedan law must apply at others; and the adjudication of disputes between members of different tribes necessitates the creation of a rough code of Bantu equity. Moreover there is little sense of solidarity with the tribe and little loyalty to the chief. The strength of Mohammedanism, the presence of a large foreign element, and the differentiation of social and economic interest as between townsman and countryman, all serve to emphasize the existence of the town as a separate social entity. At present the slow but constant migration of Hehe to and from the town serves to blur the distinction; but with the further development of urban interests it is more than possible that the situation will outgrow the ability of the tribal authorities to deal with it. It is, therefore, our opinion that in the interests of both town and tribe it would be advisable to separate them.

We have so far suggested certain issues which may arise in the executive sphere of tribal development. On the legal side, supervision is also required. We shall discuss here the problems of the native courts, leaving until a later section some remarks on the influence of European legal concepts. We believe, as we have stated,[1] that the Hehe courts are based on native custom and procedure, and that the modifications which have occurred and are occurring are those which are imposed upon them by administrative action and by certain facts of social change. We believe also that they, for the most part, administer efficient and impartial justice, but that there are some abuses, the worst of which is delay.

The administrative officer supervises the functioning of the native courts by examining their court records, by listening to complaints regarding judicial delays or refusals to hear cases, and by deciding appeals. It will not be out of place to inquire into the efficiency of each form of supervision.

The court records are useful in that they expose the honest faults of the native judges. They show where ignorance of the law, of their own legal limitations, and of the new significance of certain offences must be corrected; but they seldom, and then only inadvertently, give any material for unearthing real abuses.

[1] See above, Chapter II, section B, pp. 120–7.

Thus delay or refusal to administer justice is not brought to the notice of the European officer, because such cases do not appear on the books at all. Consequently it may be said that the records are honest, if rough and brief, accounts of the cases tried, but that they are not faithful, in so far as they are not complete accounts of all the cases brought before the courts.

The other avenues of supervision are thus essential, but they are not as effective as they might be. Complaints or judicial appeals (the same thing in the eyes of the Hehe) are seldom brought to the District Office. This does not mean that there are few cases where a litigant feels he has not received justice; it means that there are many reasons against appeal. First, as we also say elsewhere,[1] the Hehe prefer their own courts, because they understand what is happening in them, whereas they feel that the European courts are foreign, even when they intend to be sympathetic; and they are consequently feared. Secondly, there is no doubt that the fear of what may happen to them afterwards is a powerful deterrent to appeal. Thus, while practically the whole tribe knows that appeals are permitted, few avail themselves of the privilege, even when they believe they have suffered injustice.

We have suggested that, for many reasons, constant supervision of the native authorities will be necessary for many years to come. But, if such super-

[1] See below, section C of this chapter, p. 205.

vision is to be constructive rather than the mere keeping of the peace, we believe that two conditions are essential: the District Officer must be given an opportunity of acquiring an understanding of the people and gaining their trust, and more efficient means of communicating with them must be evolved.

For the first condition, we suggest that it is necessary to post administrative officials to districts for longer periods than has formerly been the case. There have been four different District Officers and several acting District Officers in Iringa since the institution of indirect rule in 1926. The consequence is that no one of them has been able to gain the full confidence of the tribe. The Hehe trust men, not offices; and if information relevant to administrative needs is to be obtained, if appeals are to be brought in as they should be, the Hehe must be given time to realize that there is one man they know and can trust. It is equally important for the District Officer to be given time to grasp the significance of the various issues of tribal administration: while a certain amount may be learnt in a short time, the full knowledge necessary to deal with the more important issues can only be acquired by slow degrees. We are aware of the exigencies of the service which necessitate transfers; but we think that, if our opinion as to the necessity for continuity of policy were more widely shared, these transfers would be less frequent.

The other essential condition is communication.

Swahili[1] is useful for the performance of routine tasks and for issuing simple orders; and, considering the fact that it is a foreign language to both parties, it is astonishingly efficient. But while many Hehe know it well and most of them to some degree, however slight, it is not sufficient for the conveyance of ideas of any complexity, except through the medium of interpreters. At present the interpretation is not good. The interpreters make honest and able efforts, but when they do not understand the general significance of the issues they are trying to explain they are apt to give a verbally accurate translation, which after all misses the main point. This fact we have proved on more than one occasion. One solution is to demand that officials learn the vernaculars of the tribes they are administering; but under present conditions this is not possible for any but exceptionally able linguists. It only remains to improve the standard of interpretation. This might be done by selecting intelligent and able natives as administrative interpreters (and not using court interpreters for all purposes, as at present). These men might be generally instructed in government policy as it affected the tribe; and thus, when occasion arose, they could be trusted to convey the real sense of what was said and to become real instruments of communication. In time, as an effective knowledge of Swahili spreads, such interpreters may become unnecessary; but we believe that, for a generation at least, they would be worth all the money and

[1] Swahili is the official *lingua franca* of Tanganyika.

time spent on them; for we do not see how the necessary changes can be effected in tribal life without a clear exchange of ideas between governors and governed.

B. *TAXATION*

The hut and poll tax at the present rate represents about 31 per cent. of the average annual cash income of the tribesmen.[1] The cash income is only a part of the real income of the tribe. Food and housing are outside the money economy for the most part, and, where the old system of obtaining products of native craftsmanship holds, certain other goods are procurable without the use of money.[2] In stating, therefore, the percentage of annual cash income which is paid in tax, there is no implied suggestion that this is the proportion of real income involved.

It may throw some light on the way the tax affects the people to indicate the annual sacrifice involved. Assuming the tax to average 9 shillings per taxpayer,[3] we can estimate approximately its equivalent in work, in produce sold, and in stock. In working for wages, the unskilled labourer may average about 7 shillings a month (in 1933). If he works near home, he need therefore work only a little over a month to pay his tax. If he works at a distance from home, he will have to pay at least 2 shillings a month for food; to pay his tax, he must therefore work nearly two months.

[1] See below, Appendix C, p. 262.
[2] See above, Chapter II, section D, pp. 150–2.
[3] See above, Chapter II, section A 2 (*b*), p. 107. This calculation is made from the polygyny estimates.

If the produce of plantations is sold to pay the tax, much depends upon the kind of produce and the time of year in which it is sold. If, as usual, it is maize, and if, as frequently occurs, it is sold immediately after the harvest, the price may be as low as 6 shillings a bag. This means, approximately, the produce of three-eighths of an acre. Assuming the average plot to be five acres, the taxpayer pays in tax $7\frac{1}{2}$ per cent. of his annual produce.

If cattle are sold, the price varies. In 1933 the average may have been as low as 9 shillings per beast; we have seen small oxen fetch only 6 shillings. If the sale of one ox would pay the tax, the sacrifice is equal to one-sixth of the herd, since the average ownership of cattle is about six per taxpayer. But this is not a true statement of the case, since some of the herd are cows, which have a higher market value. Assuming the herd to consist of four cows, each worth 18 shillings, and two bulls, each worth 9 shillings, the tax accounts for 10 per cent. of the value of the cattle.

The payment of the tax is thus possible. It is not easy, as it involves an annual sacrifice, of labour or property, of some magnitude. But it is within the means or the ability of the vast majority of the tribe, without excessive hardship. It is, of course, not popular, but it can hardly be said to cause discontent. It is taken philosophically, as an undesirable but comprehensible aspect of European rule.

The plural wives' tax, introduced in 1932, is not interpreted by the Hehe as an extra tax on the polygynist for every wife in excess of one; it is taken by them to be a tax on the women themselves. It is, for instance, a common occurrence for the man to pay his 8-shilling tax and then to force those of his wives for whom he is taxed extra to pay the 2 shillings each themselves. This misinterpretation is not made by commoners only; it is the attitude also adopted by the tribal authorities. Headmen endeavour to collect from the women; and even sub-chiefs and their tax-clerks assume that the women on account of whom the extra tax is levied are themselves responsible for its payment.

An extension of this general mistake is to tax widows and unmarried women. The justification given is that, if a woman were tax-free unmarried, she would not marry if she should then be required to pay tax. That is, the native authorities feel that the plural wives' tax will make polygyny unpopular with the women, unless they are taxed, whether married or not. This practice has been stopped for the most part; we are unable to say whether it has been discontinued completely. But the fact that such incidents have occurred is a vivid illustration of the Hehe interpretation of the tax and of their attitude towards it.

At the time of writing, the plural wives' tax is only in its second year, and no definite statement can be made regarding its future effects. But we believe that, even if continued explanations will succeed in convincing the tribal authorities that the tax is on men only, in accordance with the number of their wives, a large number of the Hehe will still continue to regard it as a tax on women; and those women will be made to pay by their husbands. Consequently we are of the opinion that it would be preferable to revert to the old system of a single, uniform tax, even if it means increasing it to 10 shillings.

The plural wives' tax is the first attempt made to introduce a graduated form of taxation. We do not believe that any other graduated form of taxation would have even its dubious success. The Hehe are not yet prepared to accept the concept that taxation should be proportionate to wealth. To them the tax is a simple, concrete obligation they owe to the Government; and the simpler it is, the easier it will be of collection. It is, moreover, difficult to see on what criteria any graduation could be based. It is obviously undesirable to discourage more extensive agriculture, by imposing a tax on cultivated acreage. To impose a tax on large houses would similarly discourage industry and reduce the standards of living. The only other measurable form of wealth is in cattle. While a tax on cattle would be comprehensible, it would probably lead to evasion. Herds would be broken up and an accurate census of cattle-ownership could easily be made impossible. And finally, any form of assessment for graduated taxation would doubtless cost more than the tax would yield. Thus all our arguments lead to the conclusion that a simple, uniform tax is better understood by the tribe, causes less difficulty within the tribe itself and is more easily collected.

C. EUROPEAN LAW

The system of law introduced by European governments affects the natives in two ways. It renders them liable to trial and punishment in the European courts for the commission of certain classes of offences; and it influences the development of their own tribal law.

Those offences which, by European standards, would be considered serious crimes cannot be dealt with by the native courts, but must be tried by European magistrates or by the High Court. Also civil cases involving property over a certain value and litigation between native and non-native must go to the European courts for settlement. Thus, the native of Tanganyika may come into contact with civil or criminal law and with European legal procedure, and may have to undergo certain punishments sanctioned by European law but foreign to his own.

Of the native attitude towards court procedure, it is difficult to say much. Very few Hehe have reached a stage of sophistication or a standard of education which would enable them to understand its principles. They know that if they are accused of certain offences they must undergo trial before a European magistrate, but that is about all. Discussion discloses that their chief reaction is one of fear. They do not necessarily fear deliberate injustice; rather the contrary; but they fear being misunderstood. Above all, the complete strangeness of the mechanism and surroundings of court procedure makes them feel at a disadvantage. This latter consideration, we suggest, is at the base of the fact that a large proportion of Hehe confess and plead guilty to the crimes of which they are accused.

The punishments inflicted act as a deterrent, but not to the same degree as in countries where they are accepted as more or less natural, or at any rate sanctioned by usage. Beginning with capital punishment for murder, we do not believe it has a markedly preventive effect. Nearly all murders committed by the Hehe are crimes of passion, and usually arise from jealousy and to a lesser degree through drink. Frequently the murderer commits suicide immediately afterwards, a way out of intolerable difficulties sanctioned by Hehe custom. We have only heard of one murder committed for gain, and that occurred in the unsettled years immediately following the War. Thus it is improbable that the fear of capital punishment acts as a deterrent to murder.

Of the lesser punishments, imprisonment is the most feared. Here we find it difficult to draw conclusions. Since the punishment is feared, it probably acts as a deterrent to the commission of calculated crimes, such as theft. But at the same time it is so foreign a punishment, and one so far removed from the Hehe concept of what is fitting, that the criminal suffers no social handicap. His family may feel shame and horror when the sentence is pronounced and while the imprisonment lasts, but upon his release the criminal resumes his ordinary position in the tribe.

It is moreover possible that the general dislike of imprisonment as a form of punishment leads to a certain amount of concealment of crime by the community. Thus, while we prefer to give no positive opinion, we suggest that the social utility of imprisonment is at least doubtful, and, if a change in the criminal code were ever contemplated, the subject would be worth further investigation.

Whipping is also a foreign punishment. We have not come into contact with sufficient cases to draw direct conclusions, and can only give native opinion. The Hehe believe that if a man has once undergone this punishment he will be less likely to offend again 'unless his heart[1] is very black' (i.e. unless he is a really bad man). But they are, on the whole, inclined to think that it is less effective than fining.

Fining, while still foreign, is more akin to native concepts than imprisonment or whipping. As we have explained,[2] the native idea is that all offences are injuries against the individual and that the injured party must be compensated. Compensation is not identical with fining, but it has this in common with it, that material property must be handed over and that the offender is thereby the poorer. All Hehe with whom we discussed the matter agreed that the possible loss of property would prevent more crimes than any other punishment. They added that, as his relatives would help the offender to pay his fine, the lesson

---

[1] Literally, liver (*mutima*).
[2] See above, Chapter II, section B, p. 122.

would be more sharply brought home to a larger group, and the offender would constantly be reminded that his fault reduced the family wealth. Their only suggestion was that the injured person should get a share of the fine—a purely spontaneous attempt to harmonize native and European legal concepts.

The principal effect of European upon Hehe law is that the latter is adopting European punishments, chiefly fining. This is partly due to the deliberate action of administrative officers. As we have seen, the Hehe know no distinction between civil and criminal law: all offences are offences against people. The administration has tried to teach this distinction. In some cases general explanations have been attempted; but the most useful method of instruction has been the concrete example. The native courts have been informed that offences such as theft and personal violence are not to be considered as only offences against individuals, and are to be distinguished from private litigation in two ways. First, the plaintiff is not to pay the ordinary court fee; and secondly, the offender must be punished, as well as ordered to pay compensation.

But this principle has been carried farther than was originally intended, and fines are frequently inflicted in what we should consider civil cases. The extreme instance was that of the sub-chief who, for a period, fined unsuccessful suitors in claims for debt. But, though not so extreme, most sub-chiefs order fines for several classes of offence. Adultery and slander, for example, are now always punished with fines, fairly heavy in the case of adultery and of varying amounts in cases of slander. This alters the Hehe concept of law: certain offences are now injuries to society as well as to individuals, and payments must be made accordingly.

This development is probably inevitable, for two reasons. The one is that the native judges consider themselves as magistrates, inferior but similar to European magistrates; and as such they both may and must fine. The other is that, once the principle is established that offences are to be punished as well as compensated, it is difficult to draw the line; and the native courts will punish whenever they consider that society is injured by the offence committed. The only suggestion we have to make is that the native courts be kept within certain bounds. Fines should not be disproportionately larger than compensation; otherwise the ordinary tribesman, whose legal concepts move more slowly than those of his rulers, will feel that he is not getting justice; and he may tend to resort more and more to the unauthorized courts of the headmen.

D. *NEW RELIGIOUS BELIEFS*

We have already given some indication of the spread of new religious beliefs, and have stated our opinion that they will destroy the indigenous religion. It remains to suggest some other results which will follow the adoption of Christianity and Mohammedanism.

Ancestor-worship is a family religion, sanctioning the intensity of the kinship bonds. It can only become a community or a tribal religion when the community or the tribe is associated with one family, in which case the ancestors of that family may become, in a very limited sense, deities of the group. This extension of ancestor-worship has obvious limits, and the possibility of a religious sanction to the social or political union of larger communities is correspondingly restricted. The acceptance of Mohammedanism or Christianity abolishes the local concept of religion and at least prepares the way for the creation of larger units, when other factors will permit. This new possibility is as yet realized only to a very small degree. A Hehe Christian, for example, will feel some sort of community of interests with a Christian from another tribe, where formerly they would have been inevitable enemies. But, unless reinforced by other sanctions, this feeling will be very small. Moreover a Christian convert frequently associates himself with the particular mission which converted him, rather than with Christians in general: 'I am a Christian of Tosamaganga' is a statement frequently heard. But this sanction to relationships with people of other tribes is significant in connexion with the economic and political factors which are creating new and more widespread bonds and uniting peoples of various tribes throughout the Territory.

Within the tribe both religions create new social groupings. A circle of converts settled around a mission station is a community united by special bonds and interests. This does not necessarily happen at the will of the missionaries; they may wish to work in an already existing community and to change without destroying it; but it occurs to some extent, nevertheless. Similarly Mohammedans, where they live together, are self-conscious social communities. They make a distinction between themselves and the pagans, wear clothes of the type worn by the coastal natives, and consider themselves definitely superior to their neighbours. These religious communities are not in hostility to other forms of social grouping; the Hehe still retain their strong sense of family solidarity, and kinship bonds cut across those of religion; hence, although growing, the communities created by new religious beliefs are not necessarily destructive of other social groupings.

There is a possibility that the new beliefs may weaken the tribal political structure. If Christianity or Mohammedanism is adopted by the majority of the tribe, belief in ancestral spirits will gradually cease, and the religious sanction to the power of the chief and his subordinates will lose its force. Moreover, adherence to a mission station may sometimes create a conflict of loyalties, which will be hard to resolve. But we merely indicate this as a possibility. It is also possible that other sanctions will increase in strength, compensating for the loss of the religious sanction.

The new religions are weakening the force of old superstitions and observances. For example, the initiation songs teach a large number of observances and avoidances associated with menstruation, pregnancy, and childbirth; a large proportion of these are now neglected by the younger generation. Many other acts of everyday life, formerly influenced by ritual concepts, are now performed without any regard to old beliefs. It used to be *mwiko* (forbidden) to cut certain kinds of trees for firewood; this prohibition is now disregarded. It is probable that religion is not the only cause of the disappearance of such beliefs; the whole tribe, and not merely the adherents of the new creeds, are affected; but it is also probable that religion is the principal factor.

Both the new religions affect family life, but in different ways. The most obvious change Christianity involves is the disappearance of polygyny. Another, equally significant, is the institution of the Christian marriage bond, with the concomitant difficulty of divorce. These changes alter the relationship between husband and wife, and ultimately between each spouse and his or her own kindred. Christian marriage, being more enduring, becomes more intimate and implies a corresponding adjustment of the other family bonds. Just how this will alter the present kinship organization it is hard to foresee. We are not of the opinion that the general form will be changed, but believe there will be a large number of minor variations within the present framework, probably emphasizing the strength of the elementary family and weakening the more remote relationships.

The disappearance of polygyny will create a new problem, that of the surplus women. To take an extreme possibility, if the whole tribe became Christian there would be nearly 8,000 more females than males, of whom at least 4,000 would be of marriageable age. Since continence is not of likely occurrence among the Hehe, there would be a large number of irregular unions, taking the form of casual intrigues or, more probably, of concubinage. This would be a poor substitute for the present essential equality of all women. It has been suggested that if the age of marriage were raised the differential birth-rate[1] would disappear, but there is not sufficient evidence to prove the point.

Mohammedanism also affects the married state, particularly as regards the legal position of women. For example, under Hehe law the widow does not inherit from her husband, while under Mohammedan law she may claim a substantial share. But there is not, on the whole, as much difference as might be expected. Mohammedanism has been spread by men comparatively ignorant of all that it implies, and the Hehe Mohammedan can combine Hehe social observances with adherence to Mohammedanism without any feeling of inconsistency.

To the individual, the acceptance of Mohammedanism means as much the adoption of a mode of life as

---

[1] It seems to be established that the preponderance of females among the Hehe is due to a differential birth-rate, not to a differential survival-rate.

adherence to a creed. The religion was spread by Arab and Swahili traders who settled in the towns after the conquest of the tribe; and to be a 'Swahili' implies both the acceptance of the Islamic creed and the adoption of the town life, though a few hundred Mohammedans continue to live the traditional tribal life. The creed they accept is a simple one, and it includes principally a vague belief in God and the Prophet, circumcision, the performance of ritual cleansings, and, where there is a mosque, the public evening prayer. Many points of doctrine are known but neglected, particularly if they clash with Hehe custom. Only a few of the strictest refrain from drinking the native beer, and the annual fast of Ramadhan is not strictly observed. There are, of course, a few religious leaders whose knowledge of the law is much greater; but the bulk of Hehe Mohammedans do not consider very closely all that their religion implies.

The extent to which the Christian creed is understood by the mission adherents varies, and any general statement is difficult. Christianity is only a generation old. Many of the first converts had little education, and it is probable that many of them have not a very comprehensive grasp of anything beyond a word-knowledge of the catechism. The younger generation have been more carefully educated; but we have not discussed religious matters with them sufficiently thoroughly to estimate the extent of their religious knowledge. A few seem not only to have a fair grasp of what acceptance of the religion implies but to show a considerable amount of ingenuity in propagating their faith within the tribe, using the vague Hehe term *nguluwi*[1] as the basis of the new doctrines. We are able to affirm from observation, however, that acceptance of Christianity does not necessarily mean the loss of belief in witchcraft, magic, and some of the more deep-rooted superstitions, a result which common sense would have predicted.

The influence of the missions is not restricted to their religious leadership: they influence their converts by social and economic leadership, and above all by their educational activities. Since, however, there are other educational institutions within the tribe, we shall discuss that aspect of their work in the following section.

E. EDUCATION

The history of tribal education dates practically from the conquest of the tribe. The Tosamaganga Mission, established in 1896, was first in the field and began its educational work almost immediately, opening a number of village schools during the following years at various places throughout the District. A village school was also established by the Government in Iringa township; but it was not until shortly before 1914 that these schools were augmented by the opening of several schools and mission centres by the Berlin Lutheran Mission. Owing to the outbreak of the War, however, these latter were never effectively occupied.

[1] See above, p. 171.

After the War, in 1923, the Italian Consolata Fathers began to develop a central school at Tosamaganga and were one of the first missions to be able to claim the government educational grants.[1] Six out-mission stations have been opened by them since 1932, and in recent years the number of their village schools has also been greatly increased. At the end of 1933 there were 125 in operation, and they plan to have 300 by the end of 1934.

The Berlin Lutheran Mission were unable to resume their interrupted activities until 1931. In that year they reoccupied the Pommern Mission, and by the end of 1933 nearly fifty village schools had been established by them in various parts of the District.

In addition to the educational activities of these two missions, the Government have their own schools for the education of the tribe. The government school in Iringa town was reopened after the War, and in 1927 a central school was established at Malangali. In 1929 the native administration opened a school at the tribal capital, Kalenga.

The educational facilities offered in these numerous schools varies considerably with the type of school. At the mission village schools, only very elementary instruction in reading and writing is supplied. Some of them, indeed, are confessedly no more than cate-

---

[1] Mission schools receive government grants for secular education, conditional on the attainment and maintenance of certain educational standards.

chetical centres, where religious instruction takes first place. One of the aims of both the missions at present is to improve the standard of education in these schools, by drafting in better-educated teachers, as quickly as they can train them at their central schools. The education at the Consolata Mission centres is of a higher standard, and aims to give a sound general instruction, extending over four or five years, in the medium of the Swahili language. The syllabus includes some reading in various subjects, including hygiene, and it is also intended to teach methods of scientific agriculture in the near future. The central school at Tosamaganga provides education in English; and various crafts, such as carpentry, smithing, and tailoring, are also taught. More advanced courses have recently been instituted for the training of teachers and for selected boys who are to play a part in the future agricultural and economic development of the tribe.

The government town school and the tribal school at Kalenga aim to provide approximately the same standard of education as that given at the lesser mission centres. The government central school at Malangali has, since its foundation, provided instruction in English, in craftsmanship, and in agriculture.

From the above, it will be noted that the general standard of education as offered to the tribe is not high. It is, however, as good as could be expected, having regard to the fact that educational development has, properly speaking, only taken place since the War. The only criticism we venture here concerns the medium of instruction. Nowhere in the tribe is instruction given in the tribal language. Tosamaganga Mission, together with all its stations and village schools, uses Swahili as its medium; and the same is true of all government schools. The Berlin Lutheran Mission gives its instruction in Bena, the language of a neighbouring tribe, similar to the Hehe language. Thus a Hehe, if he wishes to write in his own language, must work out his own phonetics and must face the possibility that no one will be able to read what he has written. It is not suggested that Swahili should not be taught; there is much to be said for teaching Swahili to every child in East Africa. All that is suggested is that it is a curious system of education which begins by divorcing a child from the language of everyday life.

The Hehe as a whole desire their children to be educated. The ability to be able to read and write is prized as an end in itself, so much so that many grown men take great pains to learn. The more difficult studies, such as English and craftsmanship, are appreciated as a means of obtaining well-paid positions. But education as a system of individual and social development is a concept unknown to them; education only appeals when it can offer immediately understood ends. Thus, where agriculture is taught, it is sometimes difficult to convince the Hehe that any good will come of it; they have cultivated the soil at home since childhood, and it is merely unpleasant though necessary work. The teaching of improved methods of agriculture is only successful when it leads to immediately perceptible profits, such as the cultivation of saleable crops. The study of such subjects as geography or history makes little appeal; and one hardly wonders, when one sees a boy or girl who has never seen a lake or a sea being asked to enumerate the boundaries of Tanganyika Territory. Nevertheless the Hehe are willing to accept the fact that such knowledge must be acquired, if only because it is a necessary adjunct of what they consider the principal ends of education.

The results of education on the Hehe cannot be more than guessed. The large majority of the children of the tribe will acquire some sort of schooling, so that the next generation will be literate; a small proportion will be comparatively well educated. We have already suggested some possible political results; there will probably be results in economic and social life as well. But the rate of change may not be alarmingly rapid. The Hehe are at once empirical and conservative. They are willing to accept anything which has proved its utility, but there is an initial prejudice against change. This combination of characteristics makes adaptation possible, but at the same time diminishes the possibility of any serious disruption of the social structure, and thus provides a sound basis for education.

F. EUROPEAN SETTLEMENT

Before 1914 the German colonial Government granted a certain amount of land to settlers in the Iringa District, but their number appears never to have been very large. From 1918 to 1925 there were no Germans and few Englishmen in the District. About this time, however, a number of alienations were made, and settlers of both nationalities began to enter into occupation. By the end of 1933, 233,910 acres of land had been alienated for the purposes of European settlement, and 139 settlers and their families were established and engaged in various branches of farming.

The principal crops grown at present are tea, coffee, heavy tobacco, wheat, and almonds. Planting is as yet in an experimental stage, and it is uncertain which crop will eventually prove the most profitable. In addition, several of the settlers are experimenting in the farming of cattle and sheep and in the sale of dairy produce.

The main effect of white settlement on the Hehe is that it affords a number of them an opportunity of working for wages near their homes. This is particularly welcome to them, because they do not like to absent themselves for long periods from their social life and from some fundamentally necessary tasks. As it is, they can go to work for a month or more as they wish, and can even break off in the middle of a month, should occasion arise. During the planting season, very few Hehe go to work, most settlers relying upon labourers from other tribes. It is possible that, were there no white settlement, the Hehe would content themselves with less money, rather than go far from their tribal area in search of work.

Settlement also gives the Hehe a ready market for their cattle and a certain amount of their foodstuffs. It is not the only factor creating a market, but, directly and indirectly, it increases the effective demand and possibly maintains prices at a higher level than might otherwise be the case.

The indirect results of settlement upon the tribe are hard to estimate accurately, but there is little doubt that it has tended to improve the tribal standard of living. In house-building, for example, shuttered windows are becoming common, and are superseding the tiny holes which were formerly the only openings other than doors; and carpentered doors are taking the place of their clumsy reed predecessors. In furnishing the house, wooden bedsteads are becoming universal, replacing the customary cattle-hides spread on the ground. Tables and carpentered chairs are coming into use, though much more slowly than beds. And clothes are increasing in quantity and quality, though this is a doubtful blessing, since it is not accompanied by a corresponding increase in the use of soap. All these improvements are not particularly the result of settlement. They were being slowly adopted before the influx of settlers. But the increase in the number of Europeans has intensified the cultural contact and has undoubtedly been largely responsible for the speed with which these innovations have spread; and it has also helped to supply the means of satisfying these new needs.

So far as we know, there is no hostility towards white settlement on the part of the tribe; rather, they seem to welcome it. The alienations of land have still left the Hehe with more than they require for their present and future needs, and adequate compensation has always been paid when householders have been removed from alienated areas. Occasional grievances, of course, arise; individuals may feel themselves the victims of wrongs; and misunderstandings, due to language difficulties, occur from time to time. But these are purely individual cases, not representative of tribal opinion, and generally prove of easy adjustment on appeal to an administrative officer. We have no evidence that settlement is regarded by the tribe other than as an advantage; and we believe that there would be a genuine feeling of regret, if it came to an end.

IV

CONCLUSIONS

THE experiment has produced a number of useful results, within the inevitable limits imposed by a restricted field of study. The anthropologist has benefited materially from the questions asked; he has been stimulated to undertake inquiries that he would otherwise have neglected, and his views on certain factors of tribal organization have been modified. The administrator, on the other hand, has obtained an insight into many aspects of Hehe culture, as a consequence of which he has been able to perform some of his tasks with a greater certainty that serious mistakes are being avoided; and in other cases he has been able to institute certain changes in tribal administration which have beneficially affected tribal life. To demonstrate this latter point, several examples may be adduced.

In this monograph, mention has been made more than once of the registration of marriages and divorces. This was introduced to the tribe in March 1933. The question of its advisability was first discussed, and it was agreed that it might play an important part in the stabilization of marriage, into which some undesirable irregularities have been entering for some time. Next, a point that had not been previously decided, it was ruled that the man should be given the marriage certificate, because, by tribal belief, it is in his interest to keep his wife; while in the case of divorce the woman was to be given the divorce certificate, since it is in her interest to prove her freedom.[1] Finally, the certificates in use were found to be unsuited to Hehe custom, and arrangements were accordingly made for forms of a more suitable type to be drawn up.

In the sphere of political organization, probably one of the most useful of the anthropological results was the determination of the position of the headmen.[2] In the past, District Officers have been inclined to regard these as useful placemen, of relatively small importance. Dismissals were consequently frequent, to the detriment of good tribal administration. In the future, with the recognition of the real nature of their tribal status, it is probable that dismissals will be less frequent and that the position of the headmen will be seen in a truer perspective; and, while no tribal official can or should be free from the possibility of removal from office in case of misconduct, the headman will at least enjoy a security not inferior to that of his superiors.

In the administrative sphere, again, it has been demonstrated that it is useful to understand the existence and basis of local loyalties. It has been shown how the Hehe are an amalgamation of many tribes and that loyalty exists to the descendants of the old chiefs whenever it can find expression.[3] In 1933 ad-

[1] See above, Chapter II, section A 2 (*b*), pp. 113-15.
[2] See above, Chapter II, section A 1 (*d*), pp. 57-78.
[3] See above, p. 23. See also Chapter II, section A 1 (*c*), pp. 44-57.

ministrative considerations made it necessary to subdivide one of the existing divisions. The questions at issue were the extent and nature of the new subdivision and the choice of the new sub-chief. It was shown that the people inhabiting one section of the area were members of an old tribe; that the areas of three headmen very nearly coincided with the old tribal area; and that a descendant of the old chiefs was one of the three headmen in the area. Administrative action was taken accordingly, and the new unit is to be established with its own tribal head. Existing loyalties are thus utilized to the benefit of efficient administration and to the satisfaction of the people concerned.

On the judicial side, a more thorough knowledge of the status of the native courts will prevent future misunderstandings between the District Officer and the tribal authorities. While the courts of the chief and of the sub-chiefs are the only ones legally recognized, yet an insight into the essential judicial functions of the headman[1] will result in allowing him to take his customary part in native litigation. There will consequently be increased efficiency in the settlement of disputes and decreased possibility of the corruption which would ensue if the headmen's courts were driven to function in secret.

A knowledge of the principles of native law has made possible a more efficient supervision of its development. For example, it has been pointed out that the principle of fining is practically a foreign concept,

[1] See above, pp. 65–9.

and that many of the native authorities do not yet fully understand its use.[1] In future, supervision of the native courts will be made with this point in mind. Undesirable or disproportionate use of fining will be checked, and a gradual education of the native authorities will be possible. Adherence to native custom will thus be enforced when government policy decides this to be necessary, and other punishments will be introduced if it is considered desirable to foster a change in native opinion regarding certain offences.

With regard to the substance of native law, it is probable that the results of this experiment have been less full than they might have been. While it is not possible for the administrator to know the substance of native law in its entirety, unless he has a complete understanding of the whole of native culture, yet a larger knowledge than that indicated by our experiment may be found desirable in future. We have possibly erred in that direction by a too rigid adherence to the principle that information is only supplied when the administrator, after mature consideration, decides that it will be useful. It is also possible that, during a longer period of co-operation, circumstances would have demonstrated the desirability of a fuller acquaintance with this subject.

In the sphere of economics, the administrator has various interests, one of the more important being the institution of measures for raising the standard of living. For this, knowledge of the economic organi-

[1] See above, pp. 207–9.

zation of the tribe has been of assistance in preventing measures being adopted which would have had little chance of success. It has happened more than once in the past that measures which were calculated to be of benefit to the Africans have failed, because African economic organization has no means of dealing with new requirements. For example, a 'plant more crops' campaign was recently instituted to reduce the chances of famine. This achieved a measure of success, but it was recognized that, under the present economic circumstances, the possibilities of increase were limited, and that, if still greater production were considered desirable, new economic organization would have to be evolved. On the other hand, such proposals as are being entertained for the future will be attempted with full knowledge of the sociological difficulties to be overcome, and with a realization of the necessity for the development of adequate social institutions to deal with them.

These examples could be added to, but it must be remembered that there has been insufficient time to test the advantages of the collaboration in all fields of application. The experiment has only been in progress for a year, and many more circumstances will probably arise for making practical tests in the future than has been the case in the past. Thus it is now realized that the spread of missionary activity creates certain problems. It sometimes happens that when a community of Christians grows up around a mission station, the primary loyalty is given to the mission rather than to the tribal authorities. The recognition of this fact will, when occasion arises, enable it to be dealt with more adequately. The bifurcation of loyalties may be allowed for, and arrangements made to suit the changed conditions; an administrative arrangement might be adopted which would give expression to both loyalties; or attempts might be made to secure the co-operation of the missionaries to maintain tribal stability. Whatever course is eventually decided on, action will be rendered more efficient by the fuller knowledge at the administrator's disposal. Similarly, with regard to one of the problems of European settlement, knowledge of the native attitude towards wage-labour should result in more effective measures to increase the efficiency of labour, while at the same time making such adjustments to suit native requirements as seem desirable. But these things lie in the future; it is better not to prophesy when we can record specific, if limited, achievements.

The preceding paragraphs may convey the suggestion that no information of this sort was ever collected by an administrator without the assistance of an anthropologist. No such suggestion is intended. It is a fact, too well known to be insisted upon, that good administrators almost invariably acquire and must acquire a mass of useful information in the course of their official duties. In some cases their results are thorough and reliable. But this does not mean that they are as thorough and as reliable as those acquired by an anthropologist working in the field. In the first place, administration has become a very exacting profession and one which allows little leisure for other pursuits; such anthropological knowledge as is acquired must come incidentally to the administrator in the course of his other duties, or in his spare time. The anthropologist, on the other hand, is enabled to devote all his attention to the task of studying native life. In the second place, the administrator, even when he has studied anthropology systematically, is seldom thoroughly trained in anthropological theory and in the exact and special scientific methods of acquiring, testing, and arranging his facts.

The points just made are stressed because they demonstrate, in no matter how small a degree, the specific and positive use of anthropology to administration. This point, important as it is, may now be passed over, and some more general conclusions indicated.

One of the primary advantages of the experiment as conducted is that it has helped to make a preliminary definition of the specific ways in which anthropology may be rendered easily capable of application. The first point to be noted is that the field of applied anthropology (that is, of anthropological knowledge capable of immediate effective and practical application) is not necessarily conterminous with the fields of interest of the theoretical anthropologist. The present experiment aimed at defining the limits of applied anthropology; and the limits suggested by the experiment are to be seen in the presentation of results. But it is certain that administrators in other tribes, faced by different problems, would demand results in other fields. Hence, to determine an 'applied anthropology', or even an 'applied anthropology for Africa', it will be necessary to conduct more experiments of a similar nature, until some measure of agreement can be reached. These points will be considered more fully later.

A related problem is the presentation of results. After some consideration, it was decided to organize the results in a way which would present as clearly as possible a systematic account of tribal life within the limits imposed by the requirements of the administrator, but without further reference to the problems which gave rise to these requirements. The other method would have been to organize the results with more immediate reference to the problems. It is possible that others will evolve an effective way of building up a presentation of results in terms of the latter method, but it was considered advisable to adopt the former method in this experiment.

The extent to which these preliminary conclusions are valid plainly indicates the utility of making similar experiments elsewhere. We believe our results to be useful as regards their application to the tribe concerned and in relation to the particular problems posed by the circumstances of the tribe in this particular year. Other tribes and other times will produce other problems. Consequently we suggest that it would be of great advantage to the science of applied anthropology if similar experiments could be made in other tribes. If the field of applied anthropology is to be properly defined (a point already mentioned), if methods for the collection and organization of knowledge relevant to administration are to be effectively developed, an isolated experiment such as this is useless by itself, and it is essential to repeat the experiment as often as circumstances permit. If this is done, the following suggestions, drawn from our own experience of collaboration, may be of assistance.

In the first place, it is necessary to work together on well-understood lines, so that any unnecessary friction may be avoided. Mr. Mitchell has mentioned this point in his Introduction, and it has been referred to again in Chapter I, where the terms of collaboration were outlined. It is repeated here, because, in our opinion, the understanding was justified during the conduct of the experiment. The general principle is that each man must be allowed the last word in his own sphere. The anthropologist may sometimes feel that his results indicate a certain course of action; he may recommend this action if he thinks fit; but, once his information and his opinions have been given, he should refrain from criticism of the action taken by the administrator; for, in making the final decision, the administrator must take a variety of factors into account and must assume the final responsibility. Similarly the administrator must accept the information as given by the anthropologist. Administrative incidents or magisterial work may produce facts which appear to modify or contradict the results presented by the anthropologist; these facts and the possible conclusions to be drawn from them should be laid before the anthropologist; but if, after further inquiry, the suggested conclusions are decided by the anthropologist to be unacceptable, the administrator should refrain from further criticism of the anthropologist's results. We believe that it is only by a complete acceptance of this division of labour that effective co-operation can continue over any length of time. Incidentally, the administrator and the anthropologist must be people who are temperamentally suited to one another. They should be willing to trust each other and to make allowances for one another; and each must be ready to believe that the actions or conclusions of the other are based on genuine and honest conviction.

This mutual agreement will be reflected by the way in which the questions are asked. They should be as objective as possible. The collaborators fell into more than one error in this respect. For example the fourth question, as originally asked, was put as follows: 'Is our system of punishment generally a satisfactory one from the native point of view?' This question was subsequently changed to read: 'What are the effects of our system of punishment? How is it regarded by the natives, especially imprisonment?' The point of the change is that, according to the terms of co-operation, it is not for the anthropologist to say whether it is satisfactory or not; he must record observable effects. It is for the Government, with the facts in its possession, to decide whether it is good or bad, or, more precisely, to decide whether action is to be taken or not.[1]

For possible future experiments, other points might be mentioned. One, of some importance, is the extent to which each collaborator should understand and realize the difficulties of the other's problems. At the beginning of this experiment, the anthropologist had no experience of administration and only a limited reading knowledge of its problems; and the administrator had only a slight reading knowledge of anthropology. Nevertheless, we believe it to be an advantage for the one to understand the other's problems to as great an extent as possible. During the progress of the experiment, the anthropologist acquired a knowledge of the problems and methods of administration by witnessing, and sometimes by assisting in, the solution of practical problems as they arose; and the administrator acquired, by reading and discussion, a knowledge of the main anthropological problems; and it is our opinion that the experiment became more

[1] On reading the above it might be inferred that collaborators are to be asked to shed most human qualities. This is hardly the case. As an individual, each man may keep and argue his own opinions and prejudices. As collaborators in a special task, for purposes of recording information or of acting on it, and in those roles only, are the anthropologist and the administrator to observe this unnatural restraint.

effective as each man's knowledge of the other's problems increased.

Without making any specific recommendations, therefore, we suggest that it would be advantageous for each partner in a future experiment of this nature to have, or to acquire as soon as possible, some knowledge of the other's task; if the administrator has had a previous anthropological training, and if the anthropologist has studied, or witnessed at close quarters, the needs and methods of administration, the experiment will probably proceed more smoothly from the beginning.

If researches are to be conducted on anything approaching a large scale, it becomes a matter of some importance to determine, within certain limits, the time that should be devoted to each tribal area. Presumably no exact statement could be made with which all would agree; moreover, in the field, anthropologists would vary in the speed with which they master the language and acquire a basic knowledge of the tribal culture. From our experience, we suggest a minimum period of eighteen months; this would allow time to make those preliminary inquiries without which no field work can be useful and would then leave the better part of a year for the close co-operation between administrator and anthropologist. Under certain conditions this time could be reduced. If the anthropologist were to make a second research in a neighbouring tribe, with a similar culture and language, he might be able to make his researches for the administration in six months. One other factor may, in the future, reduce the necessary time. If future experiments are made in sufficient number, having the same aim as this, it might be possible to arrive at an agreement as to the field of applied anthropology. No time would then be wasted in finding out what that field was; and both administrator and anthropologist would have more precise ideas from the beginning as to what they intended to do, and could get to work on essential studies at an early period. But the possibility of this remains to be proved.

One minor point, frequently faced by field-workers, remains to be mentioned. It has been suggested that an anthropologist, beginning work in collaboration with the administration in a new tribal area, should be given a status which would rank him as an official in the eyes of the natives. We do not believe that this would be desirable. In East Africa there might be a small initial advantage in possessing a status easily recognizable by the natives, but it would result in many lost opportunities in the end. African natives recognize as well as any one else that District Officers have duties which they cannot disregard, and that they must take action on receipt of certain information; therefore many facts would be, and as a matter of fact are, concealed from them. The anthropologist suffers from no such handicap. He learns many things that natives are afraid to tell the District Officer; and the accumulation of such facts is a necessary part of the information required for a true understanding of any culture. We suggest, therefore, that the anthropologist should forgo the possible initial advantage of pseudo-official rank, for the sake of the much greater advantages to come.

A number of reasons have so far been advanced in support of our plea for the repetition of experiments on lines similar to this, but up to now we have withheld that which to us appears the most convincing. The considerations so far adduced have referred, first, to the direct advantages of anthropological information in the administration of a single tribe, and, secondly, to the necessity for similar attempts to develop an applied anthropology. The third reason now suggested is that since applied anthropology appears to be of local use, it can also be of direct use to the central Government.

The policy of a central Government is based on a number of considerations, and must be laid down, with certain reservations, for the whole country under its jurisdiction. The administrator of a district or a tribe is obliged to carry out this policy to the best of his ability. He may vary some of its details at his discretion, but he cannot deviate far from its general lines. At the same time, in an experiment of this nature certain facts may emerge which, if they hold good for the country as a whole, might indicate to Government the advisability of at least reconsidering, if not revising, its policy in some particular direction. For example it might be shown by anthropological research that present punishments for certain crimes did not act as a deterrent, or that their effects were harmful to the structure of native society. The Government might then consider it advisable to change the system of punishments for these crimes. No Government, however, could be expected to do so on the conclusions arrived at from the study of only one tribe among many. Thus, while an attempt to apply anthropology in the manner described here may affect the actions of the local administration in interpreting the details of Government policy, the results of an applied anthropology in only one area would obviously have little effect on the general lines of that policy. Consequently, if anthropological research is to be utilized to its fullest extent, that is, if it is to be brought to serve the ends of administration as a whole, the research must be spread over a wide area. A sufficient number of tribes must be studied to satisfy Government that such conclusions as are arrived at are not confined to one tribe or to one district, but are of sufficiently widespread validity to justify legislative or administrative action.

Such a general scheme of research would involve not only a series of partnerships between administrators and anthropologists, but the institution of some central clearing-house for disposing of the knowledge so obtained. This clearing-house would have three main functions. First, it would deal with the information supplied by local research and would make the wider generalizations on which administrative action could be based. Secondly, it would supply relevant information to administrators faced with specific problems. And thirdly, it would formulate its own questions to the field-workers.

This last function is, in our opinion, crucial to the problem of evolving an applied anthropology. Throughout the course of this experiment, it was found that results were most useful when administrator and anthropologist fully grasped one another's point of view. The collaboration ultimately depended upon a constant interchange of ideas; and the device adopted for effecting this, that is, the formulation of specific questions, was only a means to that end. Similar co-operation would have to be established directly between the central authorities and the anthropologist. The central Government is faced with problems affecting the country as a whole and with which the local administrator is not directly concerned. It would thus require information additional to that supplied to the local official. It would therefore be the task of the clearing-house to formulate those general problems and to ask the relevant questions of the anthropologist. The collaborators in this experiment feel that the existence of some such institution would have materially added to the value of their own results.

It is beyond our scope to make any detailed suggestions regarding the establishment of a clearing-house of this nature. This would depend on the extent of the field in which the research was to be conducted, on the number of anthropologists it was proposed to engage, and on various considerations of government policy. All we wish to suggest is its necessity and the functions it would perform if it came into being.

Professor Malinowski suggests that the African Institute become or establish a clearing-house for the advancement of applied anthropology.[1] His idea is that men with practical interests are to be put in touch with men with theoretical interests, to their mutual benefit. Our suggestions are not in conflict with his, but what we have in mind is something more concrete and limited, which would serve certain immediate practical ends. Professor Malinowski's proposals have in view the continuous development of interest in the application of anthropology and in the process of organization of applied knowledge. His plan would have broader and more far-reaching consequences; our suggestions are aimed at securing more particular and restricted results. If both suggestions were adopted, these clearing-houses would be complementary in function.

Finally, it must not be forgotten that the application of anthropology to administration is not the whole of applied anthropology. Missionaries, employers of native labour, teachers, and all others who have to deal with primitive peoples in any comprehensive manner, will have their own specific problems and will require relevant information for their solution. We do not attempt to suggest the nature of the

[1] Op. cit., p. 3.

problems involved, nor the fields of knowledge necessary for these other possible branches of applied anthropology. Those will emerge only when a systematic attempt has been made to discover what they are. Our experiment has only the limited aim of evolving a working relationship between the practical problems of administration and the relevant specialized knowledge which the anthropologist is able to bring to bear upon them.

It would be possible to add to these suggestions and recommendations, but the restricted nature of this experiment does not warrant more than we have offered. It was, after all, conducted on a small scale, in only one tribe, and lasted only one year. We do feel, however, that the results obtained have served to indicate the necessity for future attempts on similar lines. We have therefore deliberately ventured to generalize, in order to stimulate discussion among those who agree with us that further exploration of the field of applied anthropology may produce results of the greatest interest to those concerned with the administration of primitive peoples.

APPENDIX A
SPECIMEN NATIVE COURT WARRANTS
TANGANYIKA TERRITORY
WARRANT ESTABLISHING A NATIVE COURT
(*Grade A*)

By virtue of the powers conferred upon me by section 3 (1) of the Native Courts Ordinance, 1929, and with the approval of the Governor, I ROBERT ALFRED THOMPSON, Provincial Commissioner, of the IRINGA Province do hereby appoint

THE COURT OF THE CHIEF OF UHEHE

to be a Native Court with jurisdiction as set out in the Schedule hereto within the following area namely:

THE ADMINISTRATIVE DISTRICT OF IRINGA

Given under my hand this Sixteenth day of July, 1929.

Sd. R. A. THOMPSON.
Provincial Commissioner,
Iringa Province.

SCHEDULE

(i) In matters of a civil nature where the subject-matter of the suit is capable of being estimated at a money value, and does not exceed in value 600 shillings.

(ii) Cases in connection with marriage subject to the limitations imposed by section 12 (*b*) of the Native Courts Ordinance, 1929.

(iii) Cases relating to inheritance which are not governed by the provision of the Deceased Natives Estates Ordinance, 1922: such jurisdiction shall be in addition to any jurisdiction conferred under the Ordinance.

(iv) In matters of a criminal nature, imprisonment not

exceeding six months, a fine not exceeding 200 shillings, and whipping not exceeding eight strokes, or for offences against native law and custom any punishment authorised by such native law and custom, provided that such punishment is not repugnant to natural justice and humanity, and further provided that in no case where fine has been ordered shall the sentence of imprisonment passed upon the offender in default of payment of fine together with the original term of imprisonment (if any) exceed a total of six months, and that every sentence of whipping shall require to be confirmed by the District Officer before it is carried out.

(v) Jurisdiction to try offences under section 9 (4) of the Hut and Poll Tax Ordinance (Cap. 63 of the Laws).[1]

WARRANT ESTABLISHING A NATIVE COURT
(Grade B)

By virtue of the powers conferred upon me by section 3 (1) of the Native Courts Ordinance, 1929, and with the approval of the Governor, I ROBERT ALFRED THOMPSON, Provincial Commissioner, of the IRINGA Province do hereby appoint

THE COURT OF THE SUB-CHIEF OF UZUNGWA

to be a Native Court with jurisdiction as set out in the Schedule hereto within the following area namely:

THE DIVISION OF UZUNGWA IN THE COUNTRY
OF UHEHE—IRINGA DISTRICT

Given under my hand this Sixteenth day of July, 1929.

Sd. R. A. THOMPSON.
Provincial Commissioner,
Iringa Province.

[1] Special jurisdiction conferred in accordance with the provisions of section 14 of the above Ordinance.

APPENDIX A

SCHEDULE

(i) In matters of a civil nature, where the subject matter is capable of being estimated at a money value and does not exceed 200 shillings.

(ii) Cases connected with marriage subject to the limitations imposed by section 12 (*b*) of the Native Courts Ordinance, 1929.

(iii) Cases relating to inheritance which are not governed by the provisions of the Deceased Natives Estates Ordinance, 1922: such jurisdiction shall be in addition to any jurisdiction conferred under the said Ordinance.

(iv) In matters of a criminal nature imprisonment not exceeding one month, fine not exceeding 50 shillings, and whipping not exceeding six strokes or any punishment authorised by native law and custom, provided that such punishment is not repugnant to natural justice and humanity, and further provided that in no case where fine has been ordered shall the sentence of imprisonment passed upon the offender in default of payment of fine together with the original term of imprisonment (if any) exceed a total of one month, and that every sentence of whipping shall require to be confirmed by the District Officer before it is carried out.

(v) Jurisdiction to try offences under Section 9 (4) of the Hut and Poll Tax Ordinance (Cap. 63 of the Laws).[1]

---

[1] Op. cit., p. 242.

APPENDIX A

ORDER UNDER SECTION 33 (1) OF THE NATIVE COURTS ORDINANCE, 1929

By virtue of the powers vested in me by Section 33 (1) of the Native Courts Ordinance, 1929, and with the approval of the Governor, I GEORGE WILLIAM HATCHELL, Provincial Commissioner, of the IRINGA Province do hereby appoint a Native Court composed as set out in the first column of the Schedule hereto to be a Court of Appeal from the Native Courts set out in the second column of the said Schedule.

Given under my hand this 7th day of October, 1930.

Sd. G. W. HATCHELL.
Provincial Commissioner.

SCHEDULE

Court of Appeal	Courts from which Appeal lies to the Court of Appeal
The Court of the Chief of Uhehe	The Court of the Sub-chief of Uzungwa
	,, ,, ,, Kalenga
	,, ,, ,, Usagara
	,, ,, ,, Idunda
	,, ,, ,, Upawaga
	,, ,, ,, Nzombe
	,, ,, ,, Mufindi
	,, ,, ,, Idodi
	,, ,, Headman of Iringa Township

APPENDIX B

SKELETON NATIVE TREASURY BUDGET
UHEHE NATIVE TREASURY
FINANCIAL STATEMENT, 1933

	£	s.
1. Surplus Balance on 1st January, 1933	1,068	1
2. Actual Revenue collected, 1933	2,392	12
Total	£3,460	13
3. Actual Recurrent Expenditure incurred, 1933	1,759	15
4. Actual Extraordinary Expenditure incurred, 1933	68	14
Total	£1,828	9
5. Surplus Balance carried forward to 1st January, 1934*	£1,632	4
* On fixed deposit in Bank	525	0
On current account in Bank	1,085	5
Cash on hand in Native Treasury	21	19
Total	£1,632	4

APPENDIX B

REVENUE COLLECTED, 1933

Details of Revenue	Approved Estimates, 1933	Actual Receipts, 1933
	£ s.	£ s.
I. Share of Hut and Poll Tax	1,687 10	2,036 0
II. Court Revenue	175 0	214 4
III. Local Fees and Dues:		
1. Liquor Licences	20 0	12 0
2. School Fees	36 0	2 1
3. Ferry Fees	15 0	11 4
4. Marriage and Divorce Fees	30 0	20 0
5. Miscellaneous	10 0	21 13
IV. Sale of Gunpowder and Caps	40 0	54 12
V. Interest on Fixed Deposit	20 18	20 18
Total Revenue	£2,034 8	2,392 12

RECURRENT EXPENDITURE INCURRED, 1933

Details of Expenditure	Authorised Expenditure, 1933	Actual Expenditure, 1933
PERSONAL EMOLUMENTS:	£ s.	£ s.
Tribal Administration		
1. The Chief	240 0	240 0
2. Sub-Chiefs	231 0	229 10
3. Headmen	300 0	300 0
4. Clerks	246 0	239 15
5. Messengers	171 0	149 14
6. Ferrymen	24 0	15 0
Carried forward	£1,212 0	1,173 19

APPENDIX B

Details of Expenditure	Authorised Expenditure, 1933		Actual Expenditure, 1933	
	£	s.	£	s.
Brought forward.	1,212	0	1,173	19
Education				
7. Teachers	66	0	61	0
8. Tribal Elders	30	0	7	0
Medical and Sanitation				
9. Tribal Dressers	123	0	122	18
Agriculture				
10. Instructors	27	0	4	17
11. Labourers	96	0	95	7
Total Personal Emoluments	£1,554	0	1,465	1
OTHER CHARGES:				
Tribal Administration				
12. Stationery	30	0	29	16
13. Uniforms	27	0	21	18
14. Maintenance of Buildings	25	0	23	12
15. Transport	25	0	22	17
16. Contingencies	15	0	14	11
17. Indigents	5	0	4	10
18. Sustenance of Witnesses	10	0		8
Education				
19. Malangali School Fees	36	0	10	0
20. Assistance to Scholars and Apprentices	32	0	..	
Roads and Bridges				
21. Maintenance of Roads and Bridges	50	0	36	13
22. Maintenance of Ferries	10	0	10	0
Carried forward.	£265	0	174	5

APPENDIX B

Details of Expenditure	Authorised Expenditure, 1933		Actual Expenditure, 1933	
	£	s.	£	s.
Brought forward.	265	0	174	5
Medical and Sanitation				
23. Drugs and Equipment	80	0	79	2
24. Upkeep of Dispensaries	14	0	1	14
Agriculture				
25. Purchase of Seed	5	0	3	0
Afforestation				
26. Re-afforestation	5	0	5	0
General				
27. Purchase of Gunpowder and Caps	35	0	31	13
Total Other Charges	£404	0	294	14
Total Personal Emoluments	£1,554	0	1,465	1
Total Recurrent Expenditure	£1,958	0	1,759	15

EXTRAORDINARY EXPENDITURE INCURRED, 1933

Details of Expenditure	Authorised Expenditure, 1933		Actual Expenditure, 1933	
	£	s.	£	s.
1. Court House for Sub-Chief of Iringa Township	50	0	42	4
2. Purchase of food for famine relief, Malangali	50	0	26	10
Total Extraordinary Expenditure	£100	0	68	14

APPENDIX C

1. A CLASSIFIED LIST OF THE QUESTIONS WHICH WERE ASKED DURING THE COURSE OF THE EXPERIMENT

THE following is a classified list of the questions which were asked by the administrator and answered by the anthropologist during the course of the experiment. As a preliminary to these questions, the administrator asked for an account of the political organization of the tribe, which was furnished early on in the experiment. Thus the questions here listed do not necessarily cover the whole field of information contained in Chapters II and III of this monograph. On the other hand, it will be observed that some of the questions asked were for information which would obviously be contained in any account of the political organization of a tribe, however brief. Where this is the case, the questions have always been asked for a special reason and to emphasize some particular point on which information was desired.

Specimen answers to three of the questions have also been included.

A. POLITICAL ORGANIZATION

1. What were the tribes existing before their amalgamation to form the Hehe unit, and what was their geographical distribution?
2. Would it increase the efficiency of native administration if the pre-existing tribes now constituting the Hehe political unit were given some form of recognition?
3. What is the nature of the chief's authority in the tribe, and how is his position regarded by his subjects?

4. What are the relative positions of the sub-chiefs and the *jumbes* (headmen) in tribal life?
5. Is the present division of the District into nine sub-chiefdoms satisfactory from the native point of view?
6. What would be the effects, and the native attitude towards, the division of Uzungwa sub-chiefdom, in view of non-native expansion in Mufindi East?
7. What have tribal law and custom to say regarding the selection of successors to sub-chiefs and *jumbes* (headmen)?
8. What is the position of the *vakalani* (minor officials) in the tribe? Under whose authority do they hold office?
9. What is the smallest unit of local government in the tribe?
10. What restrictions exist on changes of residence within the **tribe,** and movement to and from the tribal area?
11. To what extent does customary communal labour exist within the tribe? If it exists, is it subject to abuse on the part of the tribal authorities?
12. Has the religion of the tribe any bearing on its political organization?
13. (This question was asked about a particular person in the tribe. For obvious reasons, both question and answer must remain confidential.)

B. FAMILY ORGANIZATION

14. What part does the clan play in the political life of the tribe?
15. What aspects of the marriage customs of the tribe should be known in connexion with the new rule enforcing the registration of marriages and divorces?
16. What effect will the registration of marriages and divorces have on tribal life?
17. What would be the probable consequences of administrative support of the chief in his attempt to fix the amount of the bride-wealth?

18. In what light is illegitimacy regarded? Is pre-nuptial intercourse freely indulged in? Is it on the increase?
19. To what extent is polygyny practised in the tribe?

C. NATIVE LAW

20. What is the native concept of law?
21. What in your opinion is the criterion of what constitutes native law and custom?
22. Does a recognized code of native law exist in the tribe? Is there any recognized difference between civil and criminal law?
23. What kind of evidence is relied upon by the native courts when framing their judgements?
24. Do you consider that the native courts on the whole administer justice efficiently?
25. According to established native custom, what sort of men should be chosen by the chief and sub-chiefs to assist them in their court work?
26. Do any forms of punishment, as opposed to compensation, exist under Hehe tribal law?
27. Is the ratio of fines to compensation, imposed by the native courts, in accordance with tribal ideas of justice? Does the ratio as at present adopted by the native courts result in increased respect for the law, or the reverse?
28. In the administration of justice, to what extent are the native courts influenced by what they think is demanded of them by the District Officer?
29. What tribal legal formalities are required in the case of the death of a tribesman?
30. What is native opinion regarding *matusi* (abuse)?

D. LAND TENURE

31. What is the Hehe system of land tenure? In whom is the power of granting land vested? Can land be inherited or transferred or bought or sold? Are there any special rules governing grazing rights?

E. ECONOMICS

32. Do the Hehe conditions of settlement determine their agricultural methods, or vice versa?
33. What is the average annual cash income of a member of the tribe?
34. What is the attitude of the tribe towards wage-labour?
35. How much work does the Hehe woman do? Is she overworked?
36. What would be the result upon the labour done by the Hehe man and woman respectively of increased crop production or the introduction of new economic crops?
37. What are the prospects of increasing the production of crops for consumption and marketing? Is the 'plant more crops' propaganda having any effect in this District?
38. Is it feasible to start communal planting and storage of food as a safeguard against famine?
39. Are there any Hehe social institutions from which cooperative enterprises might be developed, for such purposes as the marketing of native economic crops?
40. Are there any existing groupings in the tribal social organization which have latent possibilities for future economic development?

F. NATIVE CUSTOMS

41. Have the myths and legends of the tribe any practical significance to-day, or should they rather be regarded as we regard fairy tales and traditional history?
42. What part does witchcraft, as opposed to magic, play in tribal life?
43. What are the essential aspects of Hehe female initiation?

G. ADMINISTRATION

44. Under the present system of administration, is there reasonable security of life and property and room for social and economic development? Do the natives regard

APPENDIX C

the Native Administration as native and accord it their full support and obedience as such? Is it native?

45. What advantages do the tribe derive from civilized rule?
46. To what extent is it realized in the tribe that direct access to the District Officer is always available?
47. Have you any suggestions as to how the District Officer could aid the growth of a healthy public opinion in affairs of tribal government and the administration of justice?
48. Is there oppression by the Native Authorities under the present rule?
49. From the point of view of the judicial and administrative services rendered to the tribe, do you consider that the Native Authorities can now be left to perform their various functions with less supervision than has previously been given them?
50. According to information in your possession, is there much irregular forced labour in the tribe?
51. What are the effects of including the township of Iringa under tribal rule?
52. To what extent are the native court registers faithful records of the cases which come before the courts?
53. Do natives generally know they can appeal to the District Officer? Are they afraid to do so? Would it be safe to assume from the few appeals made that there are few grounds for appeal?
54. Are the native courts developing along lines natural to them?
55. Under the present system of interpretation, to what extent do you think administrative officers are making themselves understood by the people?

H. FINANCE

56. According to native public opinion, does the present scale of Native Administration salaries bear a reasonably close relation to the importance of the various offices?

I. TAXATION

57. Is the present rate of poll tax easily paid? What proportion of the average annual cash income does it represent? Is it a cause of discontent?
58. What is the native interpretation of the plural wives' tax? Is it unpopular? Does it affect polygyny?
59. Is the graduation of the poll tax by some standard of wealth practicable? Would it be understood and accepted or would it be resented? If it is practicable, have you any suggestions as to how it could be introduced?

J. EUROPEAN LAW

60. What is native opinion with regard to our criminal law and the general procedure of our courts?
61. What is the effect of capital punishment as a deterrent to murder?
62. What are the effects of our system of punishment? How is it regarded by the natives, especially imprisonment?
63. What are the effects of whipping as a punishment? Does it act as a deterrent more than fining or imprisonment? In what light do the natives regard it?
64. In what light do natives regard offences committed under the Young Girls' Protection Ordinance?[1]

K. RELIGION—NEW BELIEFS

65. In what light are the activities of the missions regarded by the tribe? What is the extent of their influence in comparison with Mohammedanism?
66. What are the observable effects in the material sphere, and in the sphere of social organization, of the introduction to the tribe of Christianity and Mohammedanism?

L. EDUCATION

67. Is education generally desired by the members of the tribe? To what extent do they realize its importance? What are

[1] Cap. 8 of the Laws of Tanganyika Territory.

APPENDIX C

the possible results of education on the tribal political and social structure?

M. EUROPEAN SETTLEMENT

68. What are the material and social results to the tribe of the development of European settlement? What has tribal public opinion to say regarding such settlement?

N. GENERAL CONSIDERATIONS

69. Is the Hehe a typical Bantu tribe? Would the results obtained from a study of this tribe be applicable to other tribes, and to what extent?

---

2. ANSWER TO QUESTION NO. 23

In the past, when a case was brought to a headman or chief, the evidence first sought was that of eye-witnesses. For example, if one man struck another, a third party must give evidence that he saw the blow being given or that he saw marks on the body of the injured person. Circumstantial evidence, which would appear to us as being reasonable, was also accepted. For instance, the fact that a man was found in the house of a woman would, under certain conditions, be accepted as reasonable proof of adultery. In general, evidence of the kind accepted in our own courts was accepted in the native courts.

But when such evidence was lacking, divination could be resorted to. For serious cases such as accusations of witchcraft, the poison ordeal was ordered. For less serious but still important cases, ordeals of another kind were used; picking a stone from a pot of boiling medicated water is still occasionally agreed to for the private settlement of disputes, the proof resting on whether the accused injures himself or not. Other means of divination were plentiful;

some of them, still used privately, are the horn which answers questions by the way it points in the hands of the diviner; the invocation of an ancestor by a magician; and divining sticks. The main point is that no dispute was left unsettled; if direct or circumstantial evidence was lacking, magical means could be invoked. I suggest, without being able to offer adequate proof, that this worked fairly on the whole. The diviner probably interpreted public opinion by unconsciously manipulating the instruments of divination. I am also inclined to believe that there was little conscious deceit; all *valagusi* (magicians, doctors, diviners) I have met are honest and firmly convinced of the efficacy of their divinations and medicines.

Nowadays divination is not accepted as evidence, either in the informal arbitrations of the headman or in the higher, recognized courts. Direct evidence or convincing circumstantial evidence only is accepted. Those Hehe who are skilled in their own law are thus becoming more and more expert at sifting evidence, checking one statement against another and eliciting relevant facts. But the older men still complain that too many plaints fall to the ground for lack of evidence, and that divination cannot be resorted to except unofficially, to force a confession before a case comes to court.

The court relies to some extent upon evidence as to the character of the accused, particularly on evidence that he has offended in other similar cases. This is particularly important in quarrels between man and wife. Such quarrels, often ending in violence on the part of the husband, usually occur in private and, as the courts always endeavour to preserve rather than to dissolve a marriage, there is little chance of redress for the woman without other evidence.

Nevertheless, women frequently do institute a number of cases against their husbands for various offences; and even though all these cases may be lost, the fact that the wife has brought them stands her in good stead if she seeks divorce. The very bringing of them establishes the character of the husband. But, generally, evidence as to character plays a minor part; and nowadays cases are nearly all decided on the basis of direct or good circumstantial evidence.

3. ANSWER TO QUESTION NO. 33

I. Applicability of Results

The following estimates of annual cash income are based on information collected in three areas: the Wasa area, the Malangali area, and the Tanangozi area. The first two are estimates for the year 1930, the third for 1932.

The conclusions to be drawn from these figures must take into account the limited and arbitrary nature of the inquiries. First, no attempt is made to estimate and reduce to a common denominator the total income of a tribesman; every man has his house, his crops, and certain objects made and exchanged in a traditional manner. The sole aim of the inquiries was to estimate the amount of money passing through a tribesman's hands in a year. Secondly, all people who were in receipt of a regular income from continuous employment were excluded. Such people are government employees, officials of the native administration, mission employees, and regular employees of Europeans or Indians; these would account for not more than 5 per cent. of the population, probably less. If they had been included, the general average income would be slightly higher. They were excluded, because to lump together natives living the tribal life and natives who definitely depend upon regular wages would give a sociologically useless conclusion, the modes of living being so essentially different.

It should also be pointed out that these estimates are not valid for the whole tribe. In our opinion, the conditions in Wasa and those in Tanangozi are approximately the same, and these two places might be taken as representative of the inhabitants of the areas of Sub-Chiefs Chogamalinga and Malambila. From these should be deducted a certain number of people so near the tribal capital Kalenga, the mission station Tosamaganga, and the township of Iringa, that their economic position is somewhat influenced by ready markets and by the relative nearness of opportunities for labour. Without going into the details of computation, some of which can be little more than guess-work, I should suggest that the results of these two inquiries would roughly indicate the cash income obtained annually by about one-third of the adult men of the tribe. The very limited results of the inquiries in Malangali might indicate, in so far as they represent anything, the cash income of about 10 per cent. of the adult men in the southern part of the tribe.

II. Method

The results for 1930 were obtained by direct questions. The answers given were checked by conversations with informants and by general gossip. We were unable to obtain sufficient information to estimate the details of expenditure, hence our 1930 results are of income only.

Our 1932 results have been worked out with greater thoroughness. Two native assistants, trained with some care, collected the facts in the first place. In one-third of the cases we were able to check their conclusions against facts obtained from other informants. In all but two cases thus checked, we found a high level of accuracy, and we have assumed the unchecked results to be equally accurate. Five cases were rejected, because our assistants did not believe their informants were telling the truth. In this inquiry we were able to get details of expenditure in nearly half the cases.

The economic unit in each case was a man with his wife or wives and their children. This was arbitrary; economically, a wife has a certain amount of independence from her husband, and she obtains help from and gives help to her own family; but we believe the interdependence of the members of this elementary group to be greater than the independence; and, in any case, it is the nearest approach to a discrete economic unit that there is in the tribe.

III. Results

A. MALANGALI 1930.

18 cases only.

(a) Of the 18 men, 9 men worked for wages, the other 9 made the bulk of their money as follows:

Sale of cattle	5 men
Sale of produce	4 men

(b) The average income was 40 shillings per annum. One man made as little as 20 shillings, one man made 70 shillings. The remaining 16 men had an income ranging from 28 to 55 shillings.

B. WASA 1930.

47 cases.

(a) Of the 47 men, 20 went to work for wages, 27 did

not. Those who did not go to work made the bulk of their income as follows:

> Buying hides on commission . . . . 4 men
> Sale of native beer to native travellers . . 9 men
> Sale of other produce, tobacco, bees-wax, &c. . 4 men
> Sale of cattle . . . . . . 3 men
> Sale of native ironwork (to other natives) . 5 men
> Building houses (for other natives) . . . 1 man
> Practising native medicine . . . . 1 man

(*b*) Both those who went to work and those who did not supplemented their income by the sale of maize or flour.

(*c*) The amount earned annually averaged a trifle over 30 shillings. One man earned less than 20 shillings, 2 men earned over 40 shillings, and the rest between 20 and 40 shillings.

C. TANANGOZI 1932.

> 74 cases.

Of the 74 men,

> 1 has 6 wives   9 have 3 wives
> 2 have 5 wives   21 have 2 wives
> 2 have 4 wives   37 have 1 wife
>   2 are unmarried

The domestic economic unit thus varies considerably in size.

(*a*) For the 74 cases, the total cash income for the year was 2249·36 shillings, an average of just over 30 shillings per household. This, we are convinced, is a slight understatement; each individual makes a few cents here and there at intervals, and in many cases these small sums were not reported to our assistants. At a guess, one might put this

APPENDIX C

at a shilling per individual. Since the average number of wives is nearer two per man than one, and since each adult is a money-maker, we can put the average annual cash income at between 32 and 33 shillings per household. The lowest income was 9 shillings, the highest 94·46 shillings, without the possible addition of 1 shilling per individual. Three-quarters of the incomes were between 18 and 47 shillings.

(b) Of the total of 2249·36 shillings, the various sources are as follows:

	Shillings		Per cent.
Work for wages	720·00	or	32·0
Sale of produce	543·14	,,	24·1
Sale of native beer	326·85	,,	14·5
Sale of stock, cattle, sheep, &c.	506·87	,,	22·6
Other items (practice of medicines, native smithing, &c.)	152·50	,,	6·8

(c) Few incomes were derived from one source alone, but the following table gives the numbers depending principally on one indicated source of income:

Work for wages	25 cases
Sale of produce	9 ,,
Sale of beer	4 ,,
Sale of stock	16 ,,
Practice of medicine	3 ,,
Smithing	1 case
No predominant source	16 cases

(d) We were able to get information as to the expenditure of all or a large part of the income in 39 cases out of the 74. For these 39 cases, the gross income was 1076·68 shillings, an average of 28·12 shillings per household.

Main items of expenditure:

	Shillings.		Per cent.
Tax	336·00	or	31·0
Clothes, Men	277·50	,,	26·0
,, Women	220·00	,,	20·0
Hoes	61·00	,,	6·0
Other items	182·18	,,	17·0

The other items included soap, native beer, native medicine, payments of *mafungu*, cattle, maize, and clothing for children.

In the 39 households there were 39 men. Men's expenditure on clothes was 277·50 shillings, an average of 7·12 shillings per man.

There were 67 women. The expenditure on women's clothes was 220 shillings, an average of 3·28 shillings per woman.

IV. Reliability of Results

The Malangali 1930 results can hardly be taken seriously, the number of cases is so small. At best it indicates that income may be greater in that area.

The Wasa 1930 results are a better indication of income, but are none too accurate. Moreover, relevant information, such as the number of wives concerned, was not included. We can form no accurate estimate of the reliability of the figures, but believe they may be correct to within 15 per cent.

The Tanangozi 1932 results were collected and checked with more care than the others. The number of cases is a nearer approach to a satisfactory sample, and more relevant information was included in the survey. From various rough tests, we believe the figures to be correct to within 10 per cent.

The value of these facts depends upon the extent to which they are samples of a larger area. We have stated the parts of the tribe of which we consider them a true sample. This, however, cannot be proved statistically; our opinion is based upon observations of means of livelihood, access to markets, and the general standard of living, the latter with particular reference to the demand for imported goods. With the limitations of proof thus stated, we can still offer these figures as being typical of the larger areas indicated.

General conclusions from these figures are discussed elsewhere.[1]

4. ANSWER TO QUESTION NO. 64

In answering this question, the first necessity is to distinguish between initiated and uninitiated girls. All Hehe girls are initiated before their first menstruation, if possible. Before that, they are considered immature; after that, they are eligible for marriage.

A man who assaults or seduces an uninitiated girl is considered so abnormal that he is labelled a warlock, and in the olden days he would probably have been killed as such. Hehe public opinion, therefore, approves the severity with which our law deals with such cases, even though the particular punishment may not be considered suitable.

As soon as a girl is initiated, it is considered quite normal to desire her; she is as eligible for seduction as for marriage. Seduction, if the girl consents, is not an offence against Hehe law, though it is frowned upon by native opinion. It does not entail the payment of compensation, as does the offence of adultery. The latter is an offence, not against

[1] See above, pp. 152–7.

the woman nor against public morality, but against the husband, whose exclusive claim to the sexual services of his wife has been infringed. If a girl has no husband, there are no such rights and therefore there is, legally, no case. Rape is an offence, but not more in the case of an unmarried but initiated girl than in the case of a mature or married woman. Moreover, by the rules of evidence, it is extremely difficult to establish the commission of such an offence. If the girl does not call for help, she is assumed to consent, and no case arises; if she calls for help and is heard, she is rescued, therefore no rape takes place; if she calls for help but is not heard, rape takes place; but, as it is her word against the man's, the evidence is insufficient. There are obviously cases where a charge of rape could be established, but they are few. Of course, if bodily injury results, there would be a case, but again not a rape case.

Obviously, native opinion as to the provisions of the Young Girls' Protection Ordinance[1] depends upon how they see it work out in practice. If the court accepted a definition of maturity which coincided fairly closely with their distinction between initiated and uninitiated girls, they would accord it their full support. If their concepts were completely ignored, they would accept the law with resignation, as one of the inexplicable enactments of the European Government.

[1] Op. cit., p. 254.

APPENDIX D

LIST OF TRIBES PRIOR TO AMALGAMATION

The following is a list of the tribes united under the Muyinga rulers to form the Hehe tribe, together with their traditional founders and a general indication of their location.[1] Tribes which were conquered in the past, but which are not now under the rule of the chief of the Hehe, are excluded. We are by no means sure that the list is complete, although all our inquiries failed to discover any others.

	Tribe	Traditional Chief	Chief's Clan	Location
1.	Kinamuyinga	Muyinga	Muyinga	Ng'uluhe
2.	Igavilo	Kindole	Kindole	Rungemba
3.	Savila	Mandili	Nyenza	Itengulinyi / Wasa / Igongo
4.	Hafiwa	Lyelu	Lyelu	Weru / Kalenga
5.	Nyandevelwa	Mudemu	Mudemu	Ndevelwa
6.	Dongwe	Mudung'u	Mudung'u	Luhota
7.	Nyimage	Maginga	Maginga	Image
8.	Nyilambo	Kitalika	Kitalika	Ilambo
9.	Nyilole	Kihwaganise	Kihwaganise	Irole
10.	Tegeta	Nyembe	Nyembe	Lula
11.	Fwagi	Mudemu	Mudemu	Mufindi
12.	Kinakalinga	Kalinga	Kalinga	Kalinga (in Uzungwa)
13.	Chalamila	Chalamila	Chalamila	Ilongo
14.	Sagala	Mukwando	Mukwando	Usagara
15.	Sagala	Mwigombe	Mwigombe	Mwino (in Usagara)

[1] Their geographical positions are shown on the map in the frontispiece.

APPENDIX D

	Tribe	Traditional Chief	Chief's Clan	Location
16.	Nyaganilwa	Mugovano	Mugovano	Kwega
17.	Tsungwa	Njole	Njole	Kisinga (in Uzungwa)
18.	Tsungwa	Makinda	Kahemela	Musinga (in Uzungwa)
19.	Sagala	Lwafu	Lwafu	Mahenge (in Usagara)
20.	Sagala	Mwanambogo	Mulandali	Mudahila (in Usagara)
21.	Sagala	Mutalula	Wutalo	Mugovelo (in Usagara)
22.	Dekwa	Mugomahenga	Muhanga	Udekwa
23.	Dene	Mulefi	Mulefi	Luhengo
24.	**Nyam**udene	Mandongo	..	Mudende
25.	Nyamugovelo (Sagala)	Mutalula	Mutalula	Mugovelo (in Usagara)
26.	Nyang'uluhe	Mududa	Mududa	Ng'uluhe
27.	Ilongo	Nduwa	..	Mbweni
28.	Ilongo	Mugulwa	..	Ilongo
29.	Igongo	Lukungu	Lukungu	Idodi

NOTES

It will be seen that these are not all isolated tribes. They are simply political units, ruled by petty chiefs, but not constituting separate tribes. Thus there are no less than six petty chieftainates in Usagara alone, and three in Uzungwa. Some tribes are called by the country they inhabited: thus the Va-Nya-Ng'uluhe are the inhabitants of Ng'uluhe. Others are named after the ruling families: the Va-kina-Muyinga are the original subjects of the Muyinga family, the Va-kina-Kalinga are the subjects of the Kalinga. Many of the tribes, however, have tribal names as distinct from names derived from the territory or from the chiefs.

In writing the names of the tribal locations, we have departed from our phonetic rules, and have given the place-names as they appear on the maps. Thus the country inhabited by the Va-Sagala has been written 'Usagara', although the root to each is the same in speech.

INDEX

Administration, 192–201.
Adultery, 99, 102, 104, 112, 113, 189, 208–9.
Agriculture, 134–43, 158–61, 163–6, 218–19.
Ancestor-worship and ancestral spirits, 34, 60–1, 166–71, 176, 210–11.
Arab, 190, 214.

Bride-wealth, see *Mafungu*.

Cattle, 5, 31, 33, 48, 99–100, 143–5, 154–5, 157, 161–3, 202, 204, 220.
Chief, 11, 28–44; ancient functions, 29–31, 33; sources of wealth, 31–2; collection of medicine, 33–4; household, 34–6; privileges, 36, 42; present functions, 39–42; opposition to, 38, 43–4, 51. *See also* Sub-Chief.
Christianity, 60, 171–2, 209–15.
Council, *see* Family and *Vatambuli*.
Crafts, 149–51.
Crops, 5, 128, 129–32, 134, 135, 137–9, 141–3, 154, 158, 161, 164–6, 220, 227.
  Almonds, 220; beans, 5, 137, 138, 139; cassava, 130, 137, 138, 158; coffee, 220; eleusine, 5, 129, 130, 137, 138, 141; ground-nuts, 5, 137, 138, 161; maize, 5, 137, 138, 139, 141, 154–5, 157, 161; marrow, 5, 137, 138, 139; millet 5, 139; onions, 137, 154; peas, 161; potatoes, 5, 138, 141, 154; rice, 5, 139, 161; sweet potatoes, 130, 137, 138; tea, 220; tobacco, 161, 220; tomatoes, 137; wheat, 220.
Cultural change, 190–222.
Currency, 144, 151.

Diviners and divination, 169–70, 175–6, 179.

Divorce, 7–8, 21, 83, 99, 104, 105, 106, 110, 112, 113–15, 212, 223–4.

Economic organization, 17, 134–66, 226–7.
Education, 215–19.
European settlement, 220–2.

Family, 16, 83–97, 115–20.
Family council, 116–20.
Folklore, 174–5.
Forced (or communal) labour, 31, 42.

German colonization, 5, 26, 28, 37, 49–50, 152 (note), 220.
Germany, education in, 37, 44.

Headman, 21, 29, 32, 37, 43, 48, 49, 50–3, 55, 57–78, 116, 117–18, 126, 128, 224, 225; collection of medicines, 63–4; sources of wealth, 64–5; household, 65; corruption, 65; functions of, 65–70; community of, 71–8.
House-building, 145–8, 221.
Hut and Poll tax, 10, 12, 41, 56, 70, 80, 201–4.

Incest barrier, 87, 94, 113.
Indians, 154, 155, 162.
Indirect Rule, 10–11, 37, 52.
Inheritance, 85, 118–19, 213; of widows, 21, 113, 119.
Initiation ceremonies, 18; female, 184–9, 212.
Interpreters, 200.
Ivory trade, 32.

Jumbe, 49, 51. *See also* Headman.

Kinship, 78, 82–120.

Land tenure, 17, 61–2, 127–34, 220, 222.

INDEX

Law, European, 205-9; native, 16, 120-7, 225-6.

Magic, 175-84, 215.
Marriage, 97-115; betrothal, 98-9; bride-wealth, 99-103; marriage ceremonies, 102-3; polygyny, 106-12; dissolution of, 113-15.
Medicine, 33-4, 63-4, 175-83.
Missions, 6, 171-2, 192, 210-11, 215-18, 227-8.
Mohammedanism, 60, 171-2, 196, 209-14.
Money, 151-8, 201-4.

Native courts, 11-12, 29-31, 39-40, 46-7, 49-50, 52-5, 65-70, 73-4, 113-15, 123-7, 179, 192-5, 197-9, 225-6.
Native law, *see* Law.
Native treasury, revenue of, 12-13.

Ordinances:
    Credit to Natives (Restriction), 10; Land, 13 (note); Master and Native Servants, 10; Native Authority, 10, 11, 12, 22 (note); Native Courts, 10, 11-12, 40; Young Girls' Protection, 264.

Plural wives' tax, 107 (note), 202-4.
Political organization of tribe, 16, 23-82.
Polygyny, 106-12, 114, 115, 136, 140, 212-13.

Rain, praying for, 34, 54, 60, 168, 170.
Religion, 34, 60-1, 166-72; new beliefs, 209-15.
Revenue, *see* Native treasury.

Schools, 215-18.
Sheep, 5, 99, 157, 169, 220.
Slander, 35, 67, 125-6, 208-9.
Slaves, 35.
Sub-Chief, 11, 37, 44-57, 58, 59; ancient functions, 46-7; privileges, 47-8; present functions, 54-7; corruption, 55-6. *See also* Chief.
Swahili, 49, 71-2 (note), 125, 190, 200, 214, 217, 218.

Taxation, 14-15, 80, 152, 201-4; collection of, 41, 56, 70; exemption from, 50, 64.
Theft, 122, 123, 178, 208.
Tribal public works, 80.
Tribal salaries, 12, 195.
Tribes:
    Hehe, 4; history, 5, 23-6, 173-4; social organization, 23-82; kinship, 82-120; political organization, 23-8; obligations imposed on, 80-2;
    Bena, 27, 147, 154; Gogo, 27; Kinga, 154; Ngoni, 26; Sagala (Sagara), 27; Sangu, 26, 27, 28; Tsungwa, 27.

Witchcraft, 124, 175-84, 178, 215.

INDEX OF HEHE WORDS AND PHRASES

Ahele kunguluvi, 171.
Atse senga, 36.

Bwalo, 146.

Chimba, 142.

Fingamba, 130.
Funo, 25.
Fyungu, 130.

Gati, 146.

Idama, 146.

Kihwele, 77, 117.
Kilonge, 25.
Kisande, 142.
Kong'oke, 45.
Kulagula, 175.
Kutega Mutego, 178.

Ligimilo, 138.
Lilungulu, 71, 165.
Lugeleka (ngeleka), 138.
Lutambulilo, 178.
Luwungu lwa Kuhalula, 187, 188.
Luwungu lwa Kwivindi, 186.

Maduga, 25.
Mafungu, 36, 84, 85, 86, 99–103, 113, 114–15, 121, 157.
Mahiliwo, 118 (note).
Mahonyo, 129, 138.
Makologoto, 76.
Maliga, 25.
Maligo, 125.
Mbwelwa, 96.
Migunda (mgunda), 136, 157.
Mihogo, 130.
Misimu, 185, 186, 187.
Misoka, 166, 169, 170.
Mitangu, 118.
Mkalani, see *Vakalani*.
Mkwawa, 5, 24, 26, 28, 34, 36, 37, 38, 44, 45, 77, 173.

Mlagusi, 167, 169, 170, 175.
Mmepo, 168, 179.
Mpangile, 45, 46, 77.
Mudegela, 25.
Mududa, 24.
Mufwimi, 24.
Mugoda, 175.
Mugoda Mwanangifu, 178.
Muhatsa, 87, 88, 91.
Muhavi, 178.
Muhitsi, 88, 92.
Mukofi, 169, 175.
Mulongo, 84, 93, 95.
Mulugu, 25, 39.
Mulugutitso, 84.
Muna kage, 109.
Muna vangu, 99.
Muntsagila, see *Vantsagila*.
Munya inyi, 61.
Mutsilo, 84.
Mutwa, 29, 45, 46. See also *Vatwa*.
Muyinga, 24, 25, 27, 28, 39, 43, 59, 84, 173.
Muyugumba, 24, 25, 26, 33, 36, 44, 45.
Mwafi, 124.
Mwanamtwa, 45, 46.
Mwidikitso, 84.
Mwiko, 212.

Nambiko, 169.
Ndina lukani, 176.
Ng'ala, 167.
Ngawanalupembe, 25.
Ngelo, 170, 176.
Ngotsingotsi, 45.
Nguluwi, 171, 179, 215.
Nguluwi hela, 171.
Nsimo (lusimo), 174.
Nyakihuko, 25.
Nyentsa, 174.

Sapi, 6, 37, 38, 173.

Tsungwa, 27.

INDEX

Ugimbi, 96, 140.
Uhavi, 178.

Vafudasi (mufudasi), 185, 187.
Vafugwa (mufugwa), 35.
Vakalani (mkalani), 49, 51, 67, 71-8, 128.

Vantsagila (Muntsagila), 45, 46, 49, 51, 52, 53, 57, 58, 59.
Vanya mulyango, 35, 48, 73.
Vapakasi (mpakasi), 48, 72 (note).
Vatambuli (ku-tambula), 29, 47, 48.
Vatwa, 59. See also Mutwa.
Veve muvina lino, 188.
Vigendo, 35-6, 48.

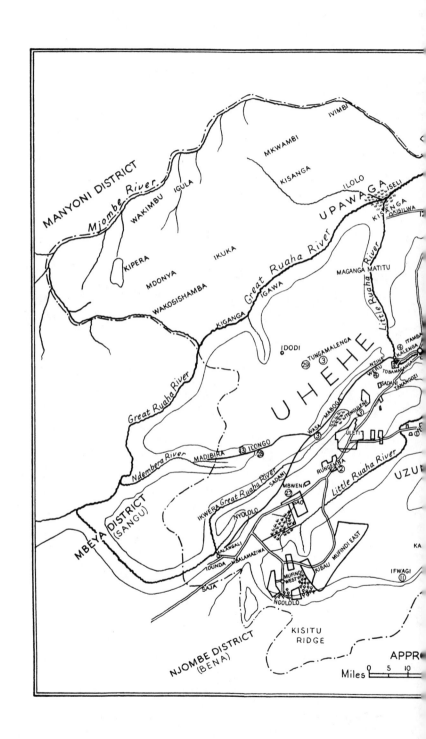

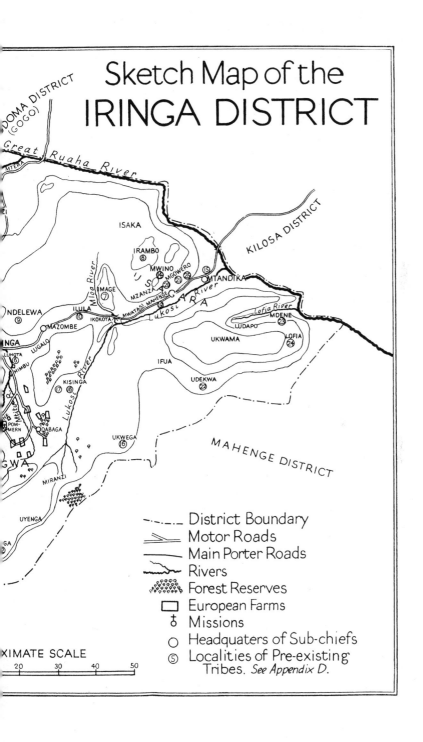